The Extreme Centre

TARIQ ALI is a writer and filmmaker. He has written more than a dozen books on world history and politics – including *The Clash of Fundamentalisms*, *The Obama Syndrome*, *The Dilemmas of Lenin*, and the novels of the Islam Quintet – as well as scripts for the stage and screen. He is an editor of *New Left Review* and lives in London.

The Extreme Centre

A Second Warning

New and Updated Edition

Tariq Ali

VERSO
London • New York

This new and updated edition first published by Verso 2018
First published by Verso 2015
© Tariq Ali 2015, 2018

1 3 5 7 9 10 8 6 4 2

Verso
UK: 6 Meard Street, London W1F 0EG
US: 20 Jay Street, Suite 1010, Brooklyn, NY 11201

versobooks.com

Verso is the imprint of New Left Books

ISBN-13: 978-1-78663-706-2
ISBN-13: 978-1-78478-263-4 (US EBK)
ISBN-13: 978-1-78478-268-9 (UK EBK)

British Library Cataloguing in Publication Data
A catalogue record for this book is available from the British Library

The Library of Congress Has Cataloged the First Edition as Follows:

Ali, Tariq.
The extreme centre : a warning / Tariq Ali.
        pages cm
 Includes bibliographical references and index.
 ISBN 978-1-78478-262-7 (paperback : alkaline
paper)
1. World politics–1989– 2. World politics–
Forecasting. 3. Center parties–Western countries.
4. Democracy–Western countries. 5. Political
culture–Western countries. 6. Capitalism–Political
aspects–Western countries. 7. Populism.
8. Revolutions. 9. Great Britain–Politics and
government–2007– 10. Western countries–Politics
and government. I. Title. II. Title: Extreme center.
 D2009.A43 2015
320.9182'1–dc23

                        2014048362

Typeset in Fournier by MJ & N Gavan, Truro, Cornwall
Printed in the UK by CPI Group UK (Ltd), Croydon, GR0 4YY

In Memoriam:
Hugo Chávez, the first leader of a movement
that defeated the extreme centre

Contents

Preface to the New Edition

We continue to live in a chaotic and confusing world. But its problems don't change – they just take new forms.

The political balance sheet since the first edition of *The Extreme Centre* was published in 2015 is mixed. The popular movements against extreme-centre policies were defeated in Greece by Syriza, the party once expected to be their champion. They were stalemated in Spain as the conservative People's Party held on to power but with Podemos slowly moving upwards while the Socialist Party divided. There is confusion in Italy as the Five-Star Movement drifts inexorably to the right. In the UK Corbyn came very close to a triumph in Britain, hampered by his parliamentarians, who are still very much part of the extreme centre.

There are glimmers of hope. The only EU state that has progressed beyond austerity is Portugal, where a left camp defeated the extreme centre and challenged the measures imposed by the EU. A fall in unemployment and a rise in GDP was the result. The governing Socialist Party (a third way, Blairite outfit) was pushed by a growing opposition to propose a coalition with the Left Bloc and the Communist Party. Both groups agreed to swallow the bitter pill, but refused to join the government, leaving themselves free to vote against it, or even to bring it down, if it reneges on its promise to oppose austerity.

In a lengthy interview with *New Left Review*, Catarina Martins, the leader of the Bloc, explained:

> So if we are in this position of occupying a terrain that, strictly speaking, is wider than the traditional space of the radical left, having to learn and create a movement at a time when successful revolutionary forces do not exist, we should always be clear when we speak to people. We cannot say to the unemployed that perhaps one day the European institutions will change. We need to tell them what we can do in our own countries to change that situation — if we don't, then the far right will do it, even if they are offering the wrong solutions.
>
> We should not let defenders of the status quo tell us that it is the European Union that is responsible for the longest period of peace and development in Europe, because that is simply nonsense. It was public investment, the welfare state, and

control over strategic sectors of the economy that made peace and development possible, not the EU ... We should not waste our time trying to make the EU a little better; we should concentrate on proposals that are practical and comprehensible, combining public control of banks and other strategic sectors with changes in labour law that advance workers' rights, and state clearly that such proposals are incompatible with the European treaties.

The honesty and courage evident here reminds me of a story from the ancient world. In Sparta, in the third century BCE, a fissure had opened up between the ruling elite and ordinary people in the two centuries following the state's victory in the Peloponnesian War. Those who were ruled demanded change because the gap between rich and poor had become too large to tolerate. A succession of radical monarchs, Agis IV, Cleomenes III and Nabis, created a structure to help revive the state. Nobles were sent into exile. Debts were forgiven. Slaves were granted their freedom and the franchise. And land confiscated from the rich was distributed to the poor (something the European Central Bank wouldn't tolerate today).

The early Roman Republic, threatened by this example, sent its legions under Titus Quinctius Flamininus to crush Sparta. Livy, in his *Histories*, gives an account of the response from Nabis, the king of Sparta. One can still feel the cold anger and the dignity, so lacking in today's politicians:

Do not demand that Sparta conform to your own laws and institutions ... You select your cavalry and infantry by their property qualifications and desire that a few should excel in wealth and the common people be subject to them. Our lawgiver did not want the state to be in the hands of a few, whom you call the Senate, nor that any one class should have supremacy in the state. He believed that by equality of fortune and dignity there would be many to bear arms for their country.

I have added four new chapters to this second edition of a book I intend as a warning. The further progress of the extreme centre is now explored by examinations of Macron's victory in France, the continued preponderance of Merkel in Germany, and rise of Donald Trump as the forty-fifth president of the United States. Some hope is found in the continued success of Jeremy Corbyn, offering some indication of an alternative in Brexit Britain. The conversations with Wolfgang Streeck, Olivier Tonneau and Andrew Murray included in the German, French and UK chapters should not be taken to indicate that any one of them shares the point of view expressed in the book. That is my responsibility alone.

Tariq Ali
1 September 2017

Introduction

Democracy is in serious trouble, especially in its European heartlands. In the United States the citizens have, more or less, accepted a broken system for over a century. A sizeable percentage of the electorate has accustomed itself to not voting, a form of passive protest and a recognition that the system is pretty much corrupt.[1] They must be smiling at Old Europe now as it slides down the same

---

1 A 2011 CBS News poll revealed that eight out of ten Americans were convinced that their elected representatives in Congress were 'more interested in serving the needs of special interest groups rather than the people they represent'. See, 'Poll: Americans Angry with DC Politics', CBSnews.com. The big banks virtually own Congress. Billions are spent by corporations on lobbying and on top lawyers employed to insert loopholes in each mildly threatening regulatory law.

path, with this exception: whereas US politics is petrified, in a number of European countries challenges to the existing structures are emerging.

As to America's two British-fathered siblings, Canada has adopted the US as its new parent and is adjusting accordingly; Australian politics has been in an advanced state of decay ever since the late Gough Whitlam, the prime minister, was removed in 1975 via an intelligence coup masterminded in London. The country now specializes in battery-farming provincial politicians of a provincial cast with impressive regularity. In all these locations, citizens deserve better.

Twenty-five years ago when the Berlin Wall came down, it was not simply the Soviet Union or the 'communist idea' or the efficacy of 'socialist solutions' that collapsed. Western European social democracy, too, went down. In the face of the triumphalist capitalist storm that swept the world, it had neither the vision nor the determination to defend elements of its own past social programmes. It decided, instead to commit suicide. This was the founding moment of the extreme centre.

In 2000, social democratic parties or coalitions dominated by them governed most of Western Europe, barring Spain. The experience confirmed that none of these parties could deliver effective policies that improved the living conditions of the majority of electors whose votes had placed them in power. Capitalism, intoxicated by its victory and unchallenged from any quarter, no longer felt the need to protect its left flank by conceding any more reforms. Even a marginal redistribution of wealth to reduce inequalities was off the agenda.

Under these conditions, social democracy became redundant. All it could offer its traditional supporters was fear, or vacuous ideological formulae, whose principal function was to conceal the poverty of any real progressive ideas: 'third way', 'conflict-free politics', 'beyond left and right'. The net result of this was either an electoral shift towards the far right (of which Austria was an early European example) or an increasing alienation from politics and the entire democratic process. In other words, an increasing Americanization of European politics offering a Tweedledee or Tweedledum choice – with a decline of the popular vote. With popular culture so heavily Atlanticized, politics could not be far behind. Nowhere in Western Europe did a social democratic party capitulate so willingly and completely to the needs of a deregulated capitalism and imperial wars as the Labour Party of Blair and Brown in the United Kingdom.

The successors of Reagan and Thatcher were and remain confected politicians: Blair, Cameron, Obama, Renzi, Valls, and so on, share an authoritarianism that places capital above the needs of citizens and uphold a corporate power rubber-stamped by elected parliaments. The new politicians of Europe and America mark a break with virtually every form of traditional politics. The new technology has made ruling by clique or committee much easier.

They are immured in exclusive bunkers accessible only to bankers and businessmen, servile media folk, their own advisers and sycophants of various types. They live in a half-real, half-fake world of money, statistics and focus groups. Their contact with real people, outside election periods, is minimal. Their public face is largely mediated via the mendacious propaganda of the TV networks, or photo opportunities that sometimes go badly wrong. They refuse to step down and talk to the people whose worlds they have destroyed.

In power they tend towards paranoia, treating any serious criticism as disloyalty, and grow increasingly dependent on spin doctors who themselves behave and are treated like celebrities. Since political differences are minimal, power becomes an end in itself and a means to acquiring money and well-paid consultancies after leaving office. Today the symbiosis between power and money has almost everywhere reached unbelievable extremes. The cowed and docile politicians who work the system and reproduce themselves are what I label the 'extreme centre' of mainstream politics in Europe and North America.

This book concentrates on the British segment, for a variety of reasons. I live here and have done so for half a century, but there are other, more important factors. This was, after all, the first country in Europe to implement the new consensus, later to be mimicked to varying degrees elsewhere, with Sweden in the lead.

Thatcher and her successors acted with the electoral support of sections of the traditional working classes, especially but not only in the Midlands, and in part with the help of oil revenues garnered from Scottish shores. Working-class Toryism was never absent in England, but it grew rapidly under Thatcher. A divided working class and an undemocratic electoral system provided the basis for Thatcher's dismantling of the 1945 reforms. She questioned the meaning of 'society' and worked to encourage individualism and consumerism.

'Each for oneself' was her motto. This notion, hardly new, and the ideological offensive to which it was coupled, led to a profound shift in consciousness, a mental and moral upheaval, which was fuelled initially by the privatization of public housing and later by the institutionalization of household debt via easy mortgages and borrowing facilities designed to aid the new consumerism.

New Labour came to power by promising little to their traditional supporters while reassuring the City of London that not only would nothing change, but that they would go beyond Thatcher and complete the task that she had set herself to take the country forward. Even before this touching pledge, a prescient former Tory chancellor, Nigel Lawson, had noted in the *Financial Times* that the tragedy confronting the Conservative Party lay in the fact that Thatcher's real heir was the leader of the opposition – a view that would soon be resoundingly vindicated.

Blair's 'New Labour' was, in many ways, the most significant ideological success of the eighties counter-revolution. It was a product of that defeat. Political differences were reduced to which party had the better advertising company and spin doctors, and whether New Labour or Tories were more responsive to market research. It is hardly surprising that this process produced mediocre, visionless politicians and reduced politics itself to pure kitsch. Insincerity reached new depths.[2]

The new systemic shift separated continental Europe from Britain, but not for long. The dystopian vision of capitalist supremacy espoused by Washington, implying the deployment of military force abroad and the redistribution of income away from the poorest to the most prosperous layers in society, would slowly, and in different ways, conquer continental Europe.

During Reagan's first term in office, low-income families lost $23 billion in revenue and Federal benefits, while high-income families gained over $35 billion. This explained the massive endorsement of Reagan in the prosperous suburbs and the Sun Belt. In Britain, more subservient than ever before, individual greed was shamelessly encouraged by the lowering of income tax

2   A classic example was Blair's response to his wife's pregnancy. 'Producing a baby', he declared, 'is much more important than winning a general election.'

(helped by the North Sea oil bonanza), along with the sale of council houses and other state assets. Financial deregulation stimulated the formation of a class of nouveau entrepreneurs, who thought little of safety regulations or trade union rights for their employees.

A hallucinatory euphoria, aided and abetted by a sycophantic news establishment, helped to cement the new consensus. A full-scale ideological assault was mounted on the old postwar settlement. Overnight, Keynesian economics was consigned to the junkyard as this new social, political, economic, and cultural consensus took hold. It was ugly. It was brutal. It appeared to work. It had to be made hegemonic: it was.

Those in the TV networks who resisted being 'one of us' were unceremoniously removed. With the help of News International's Rupert Murdoch and John Birt, director general of the BBC, an officially sponsored culture of conformity began to take shape. The situation was brilliantly summed up on a banner carried by striking South Korean workers during a general strike in the late eighties, outside a Japanese transnational with major business interests in Britain. It read: 'You Can't Defeat Us. We're Not English!'

US-style politics had made Britain a launch pad for the rest of Europe.

Germany, due to its 'special circumstances' as the spoiled child of the Cold War authorized to keep some old toys and many old personnel from the Reich,[3] learnt the art of coalition politics soon after the war. Interestingly enough, the moderate centre was transformed into its most extreme version when the warmongering Green leaders entered the government coalition to promote wars abroad and neoliberalism at home. The architect of modern Germany, Otto von Bismarck, had been fond of putting on an air of intellectual and moral weariness as he told fawning visitors: 'Let us leave a few problems for our children to solve; otherwise they might be so bored.' There is an echo of this attitude among the German ruling elite of today, exhausted by the European crisis and their own role in it.

Elsewhere, the crash of 2008 came as a huge blow to the financialized neoliberal world. Since then, France

---

3 There were other uses for such personnel. As reported in the *New York Times*, at least a thousand Nazi spies and officers were recruited by US agencies as Cold War agents: 'Evidence of the government's links to Nazi spies began emerging publicly in the 1970s. But thousands of records from declassified files, Freedom of Information Act requests and other sources, together with interviews with scores of current and former government officials, show that the government's recruitment of Nazis ran far deeper than previously known and that officials sought to conceal those ties for at least a half-century after the war.' One such agent was Aleksandras Lileikis, the 'moderate Nazi' implicated in the deaths of 60,000 Lithuanian Jews; another was an assistant of Adolf Eichmann, a specialist in devising acts of 'terror' against Jews. But hell, that was the Cold War! See 'In Cold War, US Spy Agencies Used 1,000 Nazis', *New York Times*, 26 October 2014.

and Italy have fallen. Ireland and Portugal are in a tragic state, with huge numbers of their young people emigrating to white Anglolands or to Brazil or Angola. Greece and Spain alone have produced a movement and a party – Syriza and Podemos, respectively – to challenge the existing consensus. Most of the Eastern European states are run by corrupt politicians, with capitalism the privileged reserve of criminal gangs of one sort or another.[4]

It is not a pretty picture. The few dissenting mainstream economists are dismissed as cavilling Cassandras, while political elites and central bankers are united on the need for austerity, accompanying spurious domestic wars against a largely passive 'enemy'.

The unparalleled, turbo-charged economic shifts in the Western world have not been matched by any change in its political structures, however. If, as Peter Mair wrote, the age of party politics is over, what will replace it? The ensuing decades will, no doubt, provide a model.

On the one hand, smaller nations long embedded in larger states – Scotland, Catalonia, Kurdistan – are taking advantage of the crisis and its diverse manifestations to make a bid for freedom, albeit in different conditions and under multiform leaderships. On the other, movements like Syriza and Podemos are looking closely at the

---

4 A recent study by Emily Morris, a lecturer at University College London, revealed that Cuba scored higher on all the social indices than the Eastern European states. See 'The Cuban Surprise', *New Left Review*, July–August 2014.

Bolivarian republics of South America. In both cases, worship or fear of the status quo can paralyse individuals and movements. But we live in a volatile world, and passivity is not an option.

Sifting fact from fiction is not easy today, especially in the West; but even the apologists of the system are finding it increasingly difficult to portray the capitalist societies that emerged from the ruins of the Communist system, or those that renewed themselves in the post-Communist era, as exemplars of economic stability, full employment, continuous growth, social equality, or individual freedom in any meaningful sense of the word. Having defeated its old enemy ideologically and economically, the triumphant West is now living though the twilight of democracy.

The ruling elites in the US and Europe, which so vigorously and shamelessly promoted their political system to win over the peoples of Eastern Europe, are now quietly disencumbering themselves of that very system. Contemporary capitalism requires a proper domestic and international legal scaffolding, and referees to adjudicate on inter-company disputes and property rights; but it has no real need for a democratic structure, except as window dressing. How long our rulers will bother to preserve the forms of democracy while draining it of any real content is a matter for serious debate.[5]

---

5   Two important books on this subject are the late Peter Mair's *Ruling the Void* (London and New York, 2013) and Wolfgang

Those of us who live in the West, some more fortunate than others, are citizens of a disorderly world. But a large majority of us share, in varying degrees, a new collective experience: unemployment or semi-employment, household debt, homelessness, plus the decline in quality and availability of services – health, education, public housing, public transport, public broadcasting, affordable utilities – that were considered essential in the four decades that followed the Second World War. No longer.

Even as the old Soviet state and its satellites in Eastern Europe were tottering, a comprehensive strategy was being built in Washington, DC. Its aim was straightforward: to embark on a new course for global capitalism that would reverse the declining rate of profit by removing all obstacles – countries, institutions, citizens – that stood in the way. The World Bank summarized the basics of the new economic order thus: ruthless curbs on public expenditure; tax 'reforms' (in other words, lowering taxes on the rich and extending them to the poor via instruments such as VAT); allowing the markets (banks) to determine interest rates; elimination of quotas and tariffs, thus encouraging foreign direct investments; systematic privatization of all state enterprises; and effective deregulation. Henceforth there would be no inviolable sectors in

Streeck's *Buying Time: The Delayed Crisis of Democratic Capitalism* (London and New York, 2014). Both highlight the processes at work. Mair's stinging attack on the EU provides a very strong basis for a left critique of the German-dominated bankers' union.

public ownership: the market – the corporations – would decide all.

These were the economic pillars of the dictatorship of Capital. The upshot was obvious. Politics in the old heartlands of capitalism would become little more than concentrated economics. The state that facilitated and presided over all these changes would function as the executive committee of financialized capitalism, strengthening its defences and, when necessary, intervening to save it from total collapse, as in 2008–2009.

The structurally adjusted system required a novel type of politician in the wake of those pioneers of the new order, Ronald Reagan and Margaret Thatcher. The first was a second-rate actor, operating like a brainwashed zombie and way out of his depth in the White House. Even so he learned his lines well and was lauded as a great communicator, till he began to forget which Latin American capital he had landed in and to fluff the script at home as well.

In reality, the US under Reagan was run by a cabal of right-wing zealots, an imperial politburo that took most of the key decisions of that important period. They transmitted to the world through their president, whose standing reached its height when the last Soviet leader, Mikhail Gorbachev, decided to follow Washington rather than Beijing. Reagan's successor was his vice-president, George H. W. Bush (on secondment from the CIA). He only served a single term before being defeated by the

Democrat Bill Clinton. But the legacy was safe in New Democrat hands: Clinton proved a zealous and effective defender of the Reagan revolution and much else besides.

Margaret Thatcher surrounded herself with a clique of hard-right advisers to push through the new consensus, but it was not as easy as later painted. For a start there was resistance inside the Conservative Party itself, peaking with Sir Ian Gilmour's public defiance. His book *Dancing with Dogma* was a strong defence of the postwar order. Gilmour denounced means testing in particular, with a vigour strikingly absent in later years after New Labour imposed a makeover of the opposition, transforming veteran social democrats and socialists into the living dead: John Prescott, Robin Cook, Jack Straw, David Blunkett, Alan Milburn, Stephen Byers, Harriet Harman come immediately to mind.

Domestically, Thatcher was aided by a number of factors, including an unrepresentative electoral system whereby she never had to win a majority of the votes, and an internally divided Labour Party that soon split into two. Most importantly, she was strengthened by her decision to provoke and defeat a strike by the toughest section of the British working class. Her triumph against the 'enemy within' and how it was organized has been well documented.[6]

---

6   Seumas Milne's *The Enemy Within* (fourth edition, London and New York, 2014) has become a classic on the subject, detailing the methods deployed by the state to defeat the miners.

THE EXTREME CENTRE

Externally, the war to retake the Malvinas (Falkland Islands) ended in victory thanks to the support of the Labour leader Michael Foot at home and of General Pinochet in Chile. Foot had denounced the US-backed Argentinian dictator, General Galtieri, as a Hitler (the first of many such analogies to be used in the years ahead). The defeat of the Argentinian Hitler required the help of the Chilean Hitler. The two triumphs were decisive in the canonization of Thatcher at home and in Europe. Subsequently, the 'Iron Lady' sobriquet (invented by her sycophants) became firmly attached to her name.[7] In Eastern Europe she is still regarded by the elites as the 'Mother of the Peoples'.

However, it was her own party colleagues, worried by her increasing isolation from reality and fearing electoral defeat, who brought her down. This was a shame, perhaps; it would have been far better had she been defeated at the polls. A year before she was first elected, Lord Hailsham, fearing that a left-wing Labour Party backed by militant unions was about to be returned instead, delivered a prescient address on the constitution which warned: 'There has always been a danger inherent in our constitution that elective dictatorship would take over.'

In the event, the danger (and not just in Britain) came

7   In September 2014, Spaniards were startled to learn that their right-wing government – the modernized heirs of Franco currently wrecking their country on behalf of the Troika – had decided to erect a statue to her memory in Madrid.

neither from left nor right, but from all the mainstream parliamentary parties acting in unison to defend capitalism: the extreme centre. It is an outcome of the fact that the very nature of the economic system in force precludes democratization. The contradiction between the dense concentration of capital and the needs of a majority of the population is becoming explosive. But the hollowing out of democracy is not a process that can be reversed by parliamentary decree alone. It requires mass mobilizations, popular assemblies, to create new movements and parties. They, in their turn, will need new constitutions that buttress radical democracy. This process that began in South America is now filtering through to Europe: Podemos in Spain, Syriza in Greece, the Radical Independence Campaign in Scotland – all these are pioneering a new form of politics to challenge and, hopefully, defeat the extreme centre.

1

English Questions

As of 2015, the UK is a country without an opposition. Westminster is in the grip of an extreme centre, a trilateral monolith, made up of the Conservative–Liberal Democrat coalition plus Labour: yes to austerity, yes to imperial wars, yes to a failing EU, yes to increased security measures, and yes to shoring up the broken model of neoliberalism.

Its leaders are a mediocre bunch: Labour's Ed Miliband, a jittery and indecisive figure, over-dependent on focus groups and spin, presiding over a parliamentary party (including his shadow chancellor) that remains solidly Thatcherite in inspiration; David Cameron, the Conservative prime minister, a PR confection, haughty towards the bulk of his own people while repulsively servile to Washington, Riyadh and Beijing. The Liberal

Democrat Nick Clegg barely warrants a mention. His party is likely to suffer in the 2015 general election, and we might soon be deprived of his presence altogether.

Flanked on the right by the lowest-common-denominator politics of Nigel Farage and a Ukip on the rise, this panic-ridden extreme centre tries to pander to this new right as best it can. Euro-immigration is becoming an English obsession, even though this country was at the forefront of carrying out Washington's orders to expand the EU rapidly so as to deprive it of any social or political coherence. This introduces a point rarely made by mainstream politicians or media toadies: Ukip wants independence from the EU, but appears perfectly happy with Britain remaining a vassal of the United States. Ironically, it is precisely this status that will make it difficult for any segment of the extreme centre to execute a wholesale withdrawal from Europe. Washington wants its Trojan mule in place.

Economically, the country is far from the visions of recovery and renewal promised by the Coalition and its media retinue. If anything, conditions are getting worse for the majority, while markets remain volatile. Underlying this trend is a continuing engrossment of wealth and privileges enjoyed by the rich.[1] As pointed

---

1 The facts and figures provided by Danny Dorling in *Inequality and the 1%* (London and New York, 2014) reveal an astonishing level of inequality. The book describes the ease with which the financial elite reproduces itself in Britain.

out by countless observers, while the earnings of the average employed person are either static or declining, the salaries and bonus options of the 1 per cent continue to rise.

The origins of the new politics are firmly rooted in Thatcher's response to Britain's decline. Unemployment was ruthlessly held above three million for ten years, enabling the Conservatives to push through a programme of social re-engineering – deploying state resources to crush the unions and initiate the privatization of public utilities and housing, in hopes of creating a nation of 'property-owners and shareholders' – that transformed the country.[2] The defence industry was ring-fenced while the rest of manufacturing was handed a collective death warrant. The defeat of the miners' strike obliterated any possibility of resistance by the trade union leaders and the rank and file. The triumph of finance capital was now complete. The decline of large parts of the country continued apace, and in turn, the country became increasingly restive.

---

2   The process itself was described in fine detail (and with a novelist's eye) in a set of excellent essays that first appeared in the *London Review of Books* and were subsequently brought up to date and published in book form. *Private Island: Why Britain Now Belongs to Someone Else*, by James Meek (London and New York, 2014), is essential reading for anyone wanting to understand what really has been happening in Britain and why it is in the dire state it is today.

How would the people react? After eighteen years of Conservative rule, they voted Labour and Tony Blair into office with a huge parliamentary majority, achieved by virtue of an antiquated and blatantly unrepresentative first-past-the-post system: 13.5 million, against 9.6 million for the Conservatives and 5.2 million for the Liberal Democrats. Blair had fought a slick campaign that made few promises, but traditional Labour supporters nodded their heads in appreciation and thought him wise. The key was to return Labour to power after the locust years. Many assumed that once in office Labour would return to some form of moderate social democracy, a little bit of Roy Hattersley, perhaps.

Few would have believed that Labour had become a party of war and finance capital. Yet New Labour was, as it turned out, little more than a continuation of Thatcherism by the same means. As if to stress the point, both Blair and Brown, on becoming prime minister, invited the old crone in to Number 10 for a whisky and a quick photo-op. This was not opportunism; their admiration for her was genuine.

Blair's position as leader of the Labour Party was not preordained. It was the result of John Smith's untimely death. Ideologically, Smith was a staunch European social democrat whose instinctive tendency would have been to establish close relations with Berlin and Paris. By contrast Blair styled himself as an English version of the Clinton who had recently shifted the US Democrats to the right, abandoning any pretence of a New Deal. The scale of Labour's electoral victory in the May 1997 general election surprised its leaders. They had fought a banal campaign, strong on presentation, weak on politics. It stressed continuity with the old regime rather than any serious change. Blair's presidential demeanour smacked of Bonapartism. His image was used to reassure Middle England voters that he was not too different from the Tories who had governed Britain since 1979, and that he would be a friend of big business.

It was publicly stated by Blair and his spin doctors that the trade unions would be kept at arm's length. It was also hinted that Blair and his group would like to detach the Labour Party from the trade unions altogether. A modern, democratic party had no time for old-fashioned conflicts. Ideally, Blair wanted a coalition government with the Liberal Democrats to lay the basis for a new centrist party that could dominate politics for the next fifty years. The size of Labour's electoral majority made any such desire utopian. Instead Blair and his colleagues transformed the Labour Party beyond recognition. Its slow collapse today will resuscitate the project, if the Lib Dems don't lose most of their seats.

During a lunch for big business at London's Savoy Hotel on 13 May 1996, Peter Mandelson, a close ally of Blair, stated that he favoured 'healthy profits' for companies and was not unduly bothered by the fact that this would 'inevitably lead to inequalities in incomes'. After two years of Blair, the gap between executive salaries and the average wage was the largest in Europe. This was widely interpreted as a pledge that Britain was safe for foreign investors. As a result the British economy was soon dominated by transnationals. Today, this market is five times greater than the rest of Western Europe and three times that of the United States.

Blair's ideologues were so convinced that victory had only been won because they had ditched a traditional social democratic programme that they ignored the reality of Britain under the Conservatives. The Blairites wanted to believe that the electorate punished their predecessors for their misdemeanours rather than their crimes. The decline in education and the health service, the sale of the railways and the water authorities, had not been popular. The sale of public housing to it occupants was a key plank in Thatcherite policies. New Labour had decided it was popular and promised to leave it unchanged.

Individual greed was beginning to turn to anger as people realized that they had been cheated (many had believed that Blair needed to make concessions in order to win and that once victory had been achieved it would be back to traditional social democracy). Nothing was being done to alleviate their suffering. New Labour enthusiasts do not like to be reminded that between 1990 and 1996, a million people lost their homes through repossession by the mortgage companies, while 390,000 homes, once publicly owned, were seized by those companies. Come

2009 almost one million properties were estimated to be in 'negative equity': the homeowners had paid too much for them in the first instance and could not get their money back.

Thatcher had resolved to make Britain a nation of small businesses. This was the much vaunted 'popular capitalism'. Yet by 1997, the year of Labour's victory, personal bankruptcies had 'stabilized' at 22,000 a year; 30,000 companies had become insolvent between 1990 and 1997. The 'flexible labour market' so beloved by Thatcher, Blair, and the transnationals had, in reality, made unemployment a mainstream experience. In December 1997, it was estimated that one in five men and one in eight women had suffered at least one extended spell of joblessness in their adult lives. It is this insecurity that modern capitalism, which lives for the short term, values so greatly.

If one studies the actual performance of the US economy during the same period, one sees that the model to which Blair aspired was little short of disastrous. Assuming that productivity growth – the increase in output per hour – is the most useful single indicator to determine economic health and the key to increased wealth and a growth in wages, then the situation is bleak. Over the last twenty-five years, US productivity has grown by less than half of its average rate of increase during the entire previous century. It stands at a little over 1 per cent per annum, compared to 2.2 per cent between 1890 and 1973. This means that the output available to distribute to workers – assuming that the distribution didn't change – grew half as fast as before.

On the level of wages, the picture is much worse. The distribution of income between rich and poor has polarized sharply. Since 1973, there has been a wholesale stagnation of wages. Real wages have been flat for the last quarter of a century. Today they are at approximately the same level as in 1968. By contrast, wages grew at an average annual rate of at least 2 per cent (often faster) during every single decade between 1890 and 1970, with no exceptions, not even the decade of the Depression – the thirties.

Nothing changed under Clinton. In 1998, the wages of the bottom 80 per cent of the labour force were lower than they had been in 1989, and significantly lower than in 1979. Simultaneously, the United States is the only major capitalist country where workers have actually had to increase the average number of hours they work each year, to above 2,000. This means that US workers labour more each year than the workers of any other Western country. They work 10 to 20 per cent more than Western European workers. Even the Japanese, usually top of the league in terms of working hours, sharply reduced this during the 1990s and are now working less on average than North Americans.

Inequality, too, increased in the US by leaps and bounds throughout the nineties. The ratio of executive pay to workers' wages was 42:1 in 1980; by 1990 it had doubled to 85:1, and by 1997 it had quadrupled to 326:1. In 1980, the richest 1 per cent of the population owned 20.5 per cent of the wealth. This rose to 31.9 per cent in 1989, and reached 40.1 per cent in 1997. The value of stocks tripled in real terms between 1990 and 1998, an extraordinary windfall for those who were already rich. By 2000 the top 1 per cent netted 42.5 per cent and the richest 10 per cent netted 85.8 per cent of the national wealth, leaving the bottom 80 per cent with peanuts.

This is the famous trickle-down economics of neo-liberal fantasists. When we are told the US economy is flourishing, this is true, but only for the well-off. In the United States, 25 per cent of all children live in poverty. This number is double that of any other advanced capitalist economy, except one – Britain. Where elderly poverty is concerned, the United States scores 20 per cent, but in this field, at least, it has been overtaken by its British emulators: in England, 24 per cent of old people now live in poverty.

The cold-blooded decision taken by New Labour's leaders and house academics to discard the very concepts of equality and social justice, and turn their backs on redistributive policies, marked a sharp break with traditional social democracy. Harold Wilson, Richard Crossman, Anthony Crosland and Barbara Castle, not to mention Clement Attlee and Herbert Morrison, were recast as 'loony lefties' for insisting that the state had an important role to play in regulating capitalism.

The first three decisions made by New Labour were highly symbolic, designed to show the City of London that this was not an old-style Labour regime. They had made their peace with free market values: the Bank of England would be detached from government control and given full authority to determine monetary policy.

A second determining act on entering office was to cut eleven pounds a week in welfare benefits to single mothers. The savings for the state were minimal. The aim was ideological: a show of contempt for the 'weaknesses' of the old welfare state, and an assertion of 'family values'.

The third measure was to charge tuition fees to all university students. This was a proposal that had been rejected more than once by the preceding Conservative government, on the grounds that it was unfair and discriminated against students from poor families. New Labour apologists were quick to point out that students in real need would not be charged, but the overall effect has been to discourage working-class children from aspiring to higher education.

The culture of New Labour was not simply to maintain the status quo, but to defend it as an achievement of the free market and insist that there was no conflict between corporate interests and those of working people. Almost overnight, people like the former deputy leader of the Labour Party, Roy Hattersley – a right-wing social democrat at the best of times – began to sound positively radical; yet all he was doing in his regular *Guardian* column was to reiterate traditional Labour commitments to a moderate degree of social justice.

One of the last big measures of the preceding Conservative government had been to privatize the railways, despite the fact that only 15 per cent of the population supported such a measure. At the 1993 Labour Party Conference, John Prescott, later to be deputy prime minister and in charge of transport, told delegates: 'Let me make it crystal clear that any privatization of the railway system that does take place will, on the arrival of a Labour Government, be quickly and effectively dealt with ... and be returned to public ownership.'

A year later, at the 1994 Labour Party Conference, Frank Dobson vowed on behalf of the leadership: 'Let me give this pledge not just to this Conference but to the people of Britain. The next Labour Government will bring the railway system back into public ownership.'

By 1996, with Blair firmly in control, the crystal clearness had vanished completely. Now, New Labour pledged to create 'a modern integrated transport system, built in partnership between public and private finance'. The results were less than successful. On 1 July 1999, the *Economist* – a staunchly pro-capitalist weekly – published an article headed 'The Rail Billionaires' and subheaded: 'The privatization of British Rail has proved a disastrous failure. Without big changes, things are going to get worse.' The magazine provided an example:

> Indeed, until last year, some of Railtrack's suppliers decided, in effect, which parts of the track needed renewal. Naturally, they appeared concerned less with passenger safety than with their own profits. Because they are paid by the mile, they have understandably tended to choose sections that are easy to renew rather than those that involve the most work.

In October 1999, a rail crash occurred at Paddington Station in which dozens of people lost their lives. John Prescott, then deputy prime minister, immediately went on television to insist that the accident had nothing to do with privatization. He looked shifty and uneasy as he recited the New Labour platitudes. In fact, the group of directors earning a fortune in dividends had decided that £700 million was too much to invest in ATP, the safety system that would have prevented the Paddington crash.

The public was outraged. Every opinion poll showed a large majority of citizens (between 65 and 85 per cent) in favour of renationalizing the railways. New Labour, normally very keen on focus groups and other slightly bogus marketing techniques, was not prepared to listen. In March 1998, a year and a half before the accident, John Prescott had stated: 'The privatized railway is producing windfall profits for a few people as a result of the contracts awarded by the last government. There is nothing I can do about that.'

Nothing? Rarely has a senior cabinet minister admitted the impotence of his government so clearly. The fact is, of course, that with massive public support the government could have issued public bonds to raise the money to take the railways back from the billionaires. Such a move, however, would breach New Labour's contract with big business: we create the conditions for you to make the money. The same approach was then extended to state education (opening the market to private companies) and the National Health Service, where the Private Finance Initiative would deliver hospitals to profit-making companies in return for private capital.

The one area in which New Labour found it difficult to renege on pledges made while in opposition was devolution. It was the single issue that would have brought out all the simmering tensions and hatreds within the Labour Party. The referenda in Scotland and Wales were duly held, and the citizens of the two regions voted to set up their own Parliament (in Scotland) and Assembly (in Wales). The Scottish National Party (SNP) and Plaid Cymru provided the main opposition to New Labour, and these nationalist parties were to the left of New Labour on issues of both domestic and foreign policy. In both elections, New Labour won, but by very small margins.

In Scotland, many former Labour voters deserted to

the SNP. The pattern in Wales was the same. Neither of the two nationalist parties waged an anti-English campaign; rather, both stressed the importance of Europe and a progressive social policy. Their presence partially solved the problem of a social democratic opposition to the political economy of New Labour. No similar alternative existed in England. A change in the electoral system, towards some form of proportional representation, might have compelled the fragmented forces of the left in and outside Labour to pool their resources and mount an electoral challenge; but New Labour ultimately retreated on that front as well.

On Europe, the Blair government often betrayed real confusion, giving the impression of paralysis. After an extended display of brashness in pushing the British model for the rest of Europe, an uncharacteristic silence gripped the government in the last three months of 1998. Public worries were expressed by Gordon Brown, the chancellor of the exchequer, concerned that British productivity was 20 per cent below that of tax-and-spend, muddle-through France, not to mention that of Germany. Both Blair and Brown may have been told by a kindly civil servant that by comparison with the EU countries, Britain had the lowest proportion of sixteen- to eighteen-year-olds in full-time education and one of the lowest levels of university entrance as a proportion of the age group, and ranked tenth in the educational standards of its workforce. In addition, Britain had the highest recorded crime rates of any EU country and the highest proportion of the population in prison, excepting Portugal.

The victory of the German left in the 1998 elections created turmoil in Downing Street. The crusade to bring Europe into step with Britain's low-productivity, low-education, low-tax, low-inflation economy had been stopped. After that, the only time that Blair seemed happy in Europe was when signing an agreement with the Conservative Aznar government in Spain on a joint policy for flexible labour markets – a third way for the Spanish right. Conveniently, Anthony Giddens, director of the London School of Economics, was on hand for a bit of on-the-spot guidance for Aznar's party cadres. The Spanish paper *El Mundo* greeted the Blair–Aznar deal with a front-page banner headline: 'Aznar declares war on French and German socialism.'

As far as foreign policy was concerned, all the pretensions of New Labour, as well as Robin Cook's pledge of an ethical foreign policy, quickly disappeared. The Kosovo War was simply a repeat of the tune in which Britain played second fiddle to the United States – and with far less dignity than even their Conservative predecessors. Tony Blair prancing about in his shirtsleeves while his spin doctor, Alastair Campbell, organized the Kosovans to chant 'Tony, Tony, Tony' was one of the more grotesque footnotes to this unnecessary tragedy.

In reality, Britain had little independence. Its main function was to provide mercenaries to buttress US hegemony. There, in a nutshell, was the grim reality of New Labour Britain.

Thatcherite 'modernization' was thus nurtured by Blair and refined by Brown into the creation of an overblown financial sector, a City of London protected by 'light-touch' regulation. It is shocking to note that there were fewer regulators for the whole of Britain than for the insurance industry alone in the United States. This, in turn, produced huge salaries and bonuses for the top layers and a few crumbs for the former industrial regions of the country.

Blair's subsequent electoral triumphs were used to cement the New Labour project. But the political geography, when decoded, told a different story. The figures revealed a decline in voting, marking a growing alienation from politics. New Labour's popular vote in 2001 was down by 3 million and less than the 11.5 million won by Neil Kinnock when Labour suffered its defeat in 1992. The 71 per cent turnout that had been considered low even in 1997, now dropped to 59 per cent. Only 24 per cent of the total electorate voted for another Blair government. Unsurprisingly, there were 2.8 million Labour abstentions in Britain's former industrial heartlands – the metropolitan vastnesses of Tyne and Wear, Manchester, Merseyside, the West Midlands, Clydeside and South Wales. It was traditional Labour supporters who decided that a walk to the ballot box wasn't worth the exertion.

Who were they? White workers in the old mining districts, Asians in the Lancashire inner cities, under-twenty-fives in particular. As one travelled further north the fall in turnout increased, dipping below 44 per cent in the blighted constituencies near the shipyards on Tyneside, the bleak Glaswegian council estates and the semi-derelict terraces of Salford and central Leeds; below 35 per cent in the wrecked zones of Liverpool's docklands.

New Labour victories were essentially the product of a preposterous winner-takes-all electoral system, which also distorted the Conservative collapse. The Tory vote was badly dented: from 14 million in 1992, to 9.6 million in 1997, to a mere 8.3 million in 2001. In all the major urban centres, the new Middle England that had been Thatcher's dream – non-unionized, service-sector, owner-occupier – abandoned her, either voting Labour or staying at home. The Conservatives retained only two seats out of twenty-three in Inner London; one of twenty-five in Greater Manchester; none in the urban Merseyside or Tyne and Wear regions. They were virtually banished from the Celtic periphery, with a single seat in Scotland, none in Wales. This collapse was the precondition for New Labour's uncontested rule. Slowly people began to realize that Blair's kitsch project was little different from the policies of his predecessors.

The flatulent 'third way' rhetoric had virtually disappeared by the May 2005 elections. Blair won again, but with a much reduced majority. The abstentions and the increase in Lib Dem votes (Charles Kennedy had opposed the war in Iraq and spoken at the million-plus anti-war demonstration in London) were not enough to bring Blair down. The absurdity of the electoral system was now on public display: Labour's sixty-six-seat majority was based on a popular vote of 35.2 per cent, the lowest ever to elect a government in British history. The Conservative Party, with the highest popular vote in England, had ninety-one fewer MPs than Labour in the same territory.

Blair's popularity had nosedived when he took a reluctant country to war in Iraq in 2003. The lies, cover-ups, and blatant media manipulation necessitated by the decision saw his ratings plummet. At the very beginning of the New Labour project he had promised Gordon Brown that they would share the premiership. The Iraq War made the promise into a political necessity. A weakened Blair resigned and left Downing Street. Like Thatcher, he left before being booted out by the electorate. Unlike Thatcher, who is still revered in some quarters, Blair was universally loathed except by a majority of the Parliamentary Labour Party. His successor's ramshackle government changed nothing and was soon confronted by the 2008 crash, a result of the cherished economic policies that both Blair and Brown had zealously implemented. Their political life's work had brought about their own undoing.

This system crashed badly under the stewardship of Gordon Brown, and the 'recovery' could only be temporary: failing banks were nationalized to keep the City of London afloat while squeezing the already deflated incomes of the working population, pensioners, students. There was no economic rationale whatsoever for the four-year freeze announced in Labour's March 2010 budget, but it was nonetheless adopted wholesale by the new Conservative–Lib Dem coalition a few months later. The resistance of all the victimized social layers to the austerity measures – with the exception of Scotland, which will be discussed in the next chapter – proved to be weaker, far weaker, than might have been expected. With no opposition to the measures in parliament, the lightning flashes of student revolt, ritual demonstrations and one-day strikes by trade unions had little or no impact on the government.

Political consciousness in England had by now become completely atomized and amorphous. The extreme centre's draconian cuts had only one rationale: the financial sector had to be shored up, whatever the cost. The crisis would be used to force-feed the country with 'structural reforms' to aid the £80 billion programme of cuts in social expenditure.

Ironic though it now appears, the Coalition had campaigned marginally to the left of New Labour: they promised a new bill of rights to roll back the surveillance state, an inquiry into how Britain under Blair and David Miliband colluded in extraordinary rendition and torture and, yes, even a mildly redistributive capital gains tax. Yet once the mandarins at Whitehall had brokered a deal to ensure the Coalition served its full term, all this disappeared and the two leaders moved rapidly rightwards to occupy the battlefields of New Labour and relaunch the counterrevolution in health, welfare and education that had been put on hold in the aftermath of the 2008 crash. As predicted, the results have been catastrophic for most of the country and have almost resulted in the break-up of the UK state. To see the deepening of privatization policies at the same time as savage welfare cuts was the strongest indication yet that the headquarters of the extreme centre are located deep inside a bubble world.

It was difficult, if not impossible, for the official opposition to challenge the Coalition when the government was effectively implementing New Labour policies. It is important to stress this fact, because as elections approach the sleepwalker segment of the electorate, desperate for something better, votes for the opposition in order to defeat the incumbent and nothing changes. A brief glance at the continuities of Westminster politics suggests that this is a foolish approach. In the three areas crucial to austerity, the Westminster gang are at one.

As far as welfare benefits and pensions are concerned, the trend-setter, in 2007, was the investment banker David (now Lord) Freud, anointed by New Labour to reduce the benefits bill. Freud recommended a transfer of housing benefit, incapacity benefit, disability allowance to a single, means-tested payment linked to harsh 'incentives to work'. The Coalition enthusiastically adopted the Freud plan, buttressing it with a further £18 billion reduction in payments and the downgrading of inflation-linked benefit increases. Polling organizations insist that these measures have majority support in England. If this is the case, and it probably is, then the ideological success of the extreme centre should not be underestimated.

Secondly: education. For a few decades after the Second World War, serious attempts were made to unshackle good-quality higher education from economic advantage. A system of grants was developed to provide access to higher education, and many on the Labour front bench and in the serried ranks behind Blair were the products of this system. Nevertheless, few hesitated to kick away the ladder.

In 1998, less than a year after taking office for the first time, the Blair–Brown government imposed fairly nominal tuition fees on students. This had been strongly resisted by the outgoing Conservative prime minister, John Major, as the thin end of the wedge.[3] In 2004 New Labour hiked the fees substantially, claiming that 'those who benefited' from higher education should

---

3 In a corridor of the House of Commons, Major complained bitterly to Ken Livingstone: 'Every year someone from the Treasury would put a proposal on my desk that detailed how much money could be raised via tuition fees. Every year I threw it away. Then your lot come in, and in the very first year they go for tuition fees.'

fund it themselves, and set up low-interest student loans to pay for them – fresh fodder for the financial sector. Responsibility for universities was duly shifted from the Department of Education to the Ministry for Business.

In 2009, New Labour appointed the ex-CEO of BP, Lord Browne, to 'reform' higher education. His proposals were for teaching subsidies to be cut by over 70 per cent, students to pay commercial rates on their loans, and universities to be free to increase fees at will, or compete like businesses with price-cutting to attract students, resulting in inevitable college bankruptcies and closures. All these solutions were to be implemented by the Coalition's business secretary, Vince Cable, leading light of the Liberal Democrats, who had promised to abolish tuition fees altogether in their 2010 manifesto. They were bought off as cheaply as Labour's 'left' under Blair and Brown – with low-level, but well-salaried, parliamentary appointments.

In the winter of 2010, the Coalition government made further cuts in higher education and raised the cap on tuition fees. The university students erupted. Cries of 'Tory scum' rent the air once again. There seemed to be a new mood emerging and a complacent government was taken aback by the protests, as was the opposition. For a while it appeared that this fiery and unpredictable moment might ignite a more generalized rage against the assault on the public sector as a whole. It was not to be. On the contrary, the old wines (Château Thatcher 1979 and Nouveau Blair 1997) blended in smoothly with the plastic-bottled plonk (Cameron–Clegg 2010).

The students occupied, sang, blogged, facebooked, tweeted and marched to show their contempt for the politicians who had lied to them. The Prince of Wales and his consort saw all this from close up as their car was briefly surrounded by young men and women chanting 'Parasites', a far cry from the sycophancy to which they have become accustomed. It was this movement that gave a majority of Clegg's and Cable's Lib-Dem parliamentarians the courage to vote against, abstain or absent themselves from the Commons on the day the measures went through. The fires lit in Parliament Square by the students to keep warm had turned up the heat on a rotten coalition.

A hard-faced Cameron had boasted to his European counterparts that England was a politico-economic Guantánamo where anything went. The images from London were the first sign that notwithstanding the tactics deployed by the Metropolitan Police, a real opposition could be constructed, not immediately but in the years ahead.

Parliament approved the new tuition fees and the movement subsided. Student life returned to normal, but some of the seeds sown in the snow of that year will sprout again. One of the noticeable features of the student movement was that, like their Conservative equivalents, New Labour students played no part in it at all. A party cloned from the top down while in power now found itself stranded in opposition. The continuities – Thatcher–Blair/Brown–Cameron – were too stark to be ignored or forgotten.

Had New Labour suffered a meltdown in 2010–11 a new debate might have been possible, but the rump had survived. The dominant mood within the Labour leadership was one of masterly inactivity. They would snipe at the government from the sidelines, expose its bald patches when possible, and bide their time till they were returned to power.

The two principal competitors for the leadership were brothers, David and Ed Miliband. Both were insiders. Both had climbed the ladder via the party/think-tank bureaucracy. Both had risen rapidly, as senior epigones to Blair and Brown respectively. Subsequently both were parachuted into safe working-class constituencies in the North. Each was given a job in successive cabinets, David Miliband becoming foreign secretary under Gordon Brown, while his younger brother was named minister for the environment. Leaving aside the novelty of a fratricidal conflict, the real question was not one of primogeniture but what they represented politically. Did they differ at all?

The older Miliband modelled himself on Blair, both politically and in his body language – jacket on shoulder, winking at journalists, and so on – and it was this merging of his identity with that of his leader that probably lost him the contest. He would have, his party colleagues felt, been a perfect successor, wiping out memories of grumpy old Brown and leading the way to victory. David Miliband did win a majority of the parliamentary party and the constituencies, but failed to obtain enough union votes to be elected. It was the unions that won the day for his brother. But too many illusions were vested in Ed Miliband. Incredibly, his triumph was even perceived by some on the left as the end of New Labour and a return to a better past.[4]

The corporate press obliged with absurd headlines referring to him as 'Red Ed', and a great many columns were written bemoaning the fact that his brother had lost. Both men were part of a middle generation that had spent its best years (wasted them, in my opinion) under Blair and Brown. The younger generation, particularly in Scotland, was both alienated from politics and instinctively more radical. As it grows to political maturity it is unlikely to be attracted to what is on offer.

---

4 Seumas Milne in the *Guardian* regarded it as 'a significant shift beyond New Labour politics' – 'that he represents a real change is not in question' – and 'an unmistakeable breach in the stifling neoliberal consensus that has dominated British politics'. Miliband's maiden speech as opposition leader – pledging to stand with the Cameron–Clegg government on Afghanistan – and his Blairite shadow cabinet, not to mention supporting the fundamentals of austerity, should have banished such delusions.

The Trough

It's hardly a secret that many a New Labour minister cele-brated the party's new turn and its startling change of register in 1997 by enriching themselves. Conservative ministers and civil servants were, of course, not new to this process.[5]

The list below is far from complete, but the trend that it symbolizes is clear enough, and not just in relation to the health industry. The symbiosis of big money and minimalist politics has reached unprecedented heights. This is the mate-rial basis for the politics of the extreme centre. And in case any members of the current 'opposition' front bench are drooling over future possibilities, it should be made clear to them that there is a prerequisite. They have to be in power before they receive any largesse. Once there, however, they could study the examples set out below:

Tony Blair, prime minister 1997–2007
Political parties usually rot from the head down. Where else to start than with Blair, whose urge to 'reform', 'modernize'

---

5   Indeed, Thatcher had advised Mikhail Gorbachev that one way of preventing corruption within the bureaucracy was to ensure that jobs were available in the private sector, advice that the naïve Soviet leader took to heart. When he was forcibly retired, alas, none of the Russian oligarchs were prepared to play ball. It was Louis Vuitton who came to the rescue by providing him with an advertising gig, and huge lecture fees were lined up in the US as a tiny thank you for what he had done to boost global capitalism.

and wreck the National Health Service led to what was in effect the creation of a National Wealth Service (NWS) for cronies and ministers alike? The health industry tycoons are generous to their friends.

It may be said of Blair himself that rarely, if ever, has a British prime minister accumulated so much capital so quickly since leaving office. His fortune is estimated at anything between £40 and £60 million. An exact estimate is difficult, because of the maze of companies he has set up precisely to conceal how much loot is pouring in and from what source. A sinecure from Yale, a PR consultancy from Kazakhstan, close ties with the odd Ukrainian oligarch, freebies from Israel and much more besides. It's all part of a day's work.

The material related to his finances alone would fill an entire book. Reports in the *Financial Times*, the *Guardian* and the *Sunday Telegraph* concur on most of the facts. The latter paper reported in 2013 that:

Mr Blair has two separate trading arms, Firerush Ventures and Windrush Ventures, which consist of a series of limited companies, limited partnerships and limited liability partnerships.

The latest accounts show that one of those companies, Windrush Ventures Ltd, had an income of more than £16 million and profits of £3.6 million for the year ending 31 March 2012. Profits more than trebled in that time and turnover was up £4 million on the previous year's accounts.

Windrush Ventures paid total tax of just over £900,000

with more than £12.5 million written off as administrative expenses. The group's wage bill is £2.3 million, meaning that more than £10 million of expenses is unexplained in the annual accounts.[6]

Given his obsession with money, one might think that he would have given up on heaven, but his competitive instincts and biblical literalism were strong. NATO had destroyed so many camels in the Arab deserts over several wars that the survivors, he must have convinced himself, could not possibly pass through the eye of a needle.

A public conversion to Catholicism followed his departure from Number 10. He kissed the pontiff's hand in Rome, but was told off for the Iraq War nonetheless. Nor did the trip to the Vatican alter his open breach of a Commandment. Having stationed himself and his party for so long in Rupert Murdoch's posterior, news that his own nether regions were being admired by Mrs Wendi Murdoch – an infatuation that might be used in court if divorce proceedings took place – shocked even a few sycophants.[7]

---

6   Robert Mendick and Edward Malnick, 'Tony Blair Widens His Web Via the Stock Markets', *Sunday Telegraph*, 13 January 2013.

7   'The passionate note surfaced amid the flotsam of a shipwrecked marriage. It was written in broken English by a woman to herself, pouring out her love for a man called Tony. "Oh, shit, oh, shit," she wrote. "Whatever why I'm so so missing Tony. Because he is so so charming and his clothes are so good. He has such good

With Blair as the model, his cabinet had a hard act to follow and we must give them credit for trying.

Jack Straw, member of Blair and Brown's cabinets 1997–2010

In 1968, Jack was president of the National Union of Students and kept himself safe from the turbulence of the period. He was a middle-of-the-road social democrat, close to members of the Wilson cabinet and ambitious, but not excessively so. He had few illusions regarding himself and it seemed even in the old days that the presidency of the NUS was the highest rung of any ladder that he would reach.

His politics, to be fair, didn't change all that much in later years, though even he must have felt slightly nauseated with himself for repeating all the whoppers invented by Blair and his spin doctors to force the country to join Bush's war on Iraq. Straw lied, and from his expression it was easy to tell he knew that he had lied. What else could a poor foreign secretary do? Resign? The strain of regularly deceiving the public must have been terrible. So why begrudge him a bit of money?

It is well known that the Saudi state usually pays gener-ous pensions to retiring British prime ministers and foreign

---

body and he has really really good legs Butt … And he is slim tall and good skin. Pierce blue eyes which I love. Love his eyes. Also I love his power on the stage … and what else and what else and what else …" ' *Vanity Fair*, March 2014.

secretaries (officially in return for addressing seminars attended by a dozen or so officials, half of whom are asleep and the other half busy texting minions about their evening requirements) for services rendered. Did Straw miss out on Saudi largesse?

In any event, April 2011 was a happy month for the former cabinet minister. Straw was appointed as a consultant to ED&F Man Holdings Ltd, a British company based in London specializing in the production and trading of commodities including sugar, molasses and animal feed, which helped provide the former Home Office boss and later foreign secretary with some pocket money: £30,000 a year. Straw's explanation left out the real reasons for the benevolence: 'There are 168 hours in the week, and I will work in Blackburn for at least sixty and maybe sleep for fifty. Providing there's no conflict, I have long taken the view that I am not against people doing other things. I had two jobs as a minister. I think it's really important that politicians are involved with the outside world.'

Alan Milburn, health secretary 1998–2003

Young Alan was a scruffy, no-good ultra-lefty flirting endlessly with far-left politics, and not just the politics. He worked in a radical bookstore, in downtown Newcastle, called 'Days of Hope' after Ken Loach's wonderful BBC plays. Why trade-union activists who visited the shop dubbed it 'Haze of Dope' we will never know. Might the haze have kindled Milburn's interest in health?

What we do know is that when he sold out he did so in style, bidding to outdo even Blair and Mandelson in their appreciation of neoliberal politics and big money. This was no easy task, and unsurprisingly he failed. But he didn't do too badly. After a five-year spell as health secretary he collected his debts with alacrity, becoming a director of Covidien, which describes itself as a '$10 billion global healthcare products leader'.

He is also a member of LloydsPharmacy's Healthcare Advisory Panel and sits on the European advisory panel of leading private equity firm Bridgepoint, which specializes in ... you guessed it, healthcare investments. Milburn declared his income from these juicy appointments as over £30,000 a year from Bridgepoint; over £25,000 from LloydsPharmacy; nothing listed for Covidien, and over £20,000 as an adviser to Pepsico.

Charles Clarke, education secretary 2002–2004, home secretary 2004–2006

Charles Clarke was appointed in 2006 as a non-executive director of the LJ Group, which supplies teaching materials and equipment to schools and training services, including through the government's Building Schools for the Future programme, which Clarke initiated as education and skills secretary in February 2004. Clarke is a consultant on public sector reform to KPMG, for whom he wrote a booklet promoting the use of co-payments – service user contributions – to the NHS and other public services. He also advises Charles Street Securities investment bankers/private equity fund managers. In addition, Clarke is a consultant to Beachcroft LLP, a legal firm that specializes in advising PFI/ PPP deals. How much in total? We don't know.

Patricia Hewitt, health secretary 2005–2007

Patricia Hewitt didn't waste too much time once her protector left 10 Downing Street. Long ago she served as secretary of the National Council for Civil Liberties (now known as Liberty) but more lucrative secretaryships of state awaited someone with her talents. She is currently senior adviser to Cinven, a private-equity-backed private hospitals and health care group, and is paid £55,000 per annum for her obviously valuable advice. She is also a special consultant to Alliance Boots, owned by private equity firm KKR. The consultancy payment is rather on the stingy side at £45,000 a year, but then we don't know what exactly she does for them, if anything.

And that's not all. In March 2008, Hewitt was appointed a director of BT Group, which provides business outsourcing, IT and telecoms services to a range of public bodies. Hewitt established the telecoms and media regulator Ofcom in an earlier role as secretary of state for trade and industry, and was in charge of the National Programme for IT – in which BT won one of the largest contracts – while secretary of state for health. According to BT's submission of details to the US Securities and Exchange Commission, Hewitt was paid an initial £60,000, but with an expected increase as she takes on more responsibilities, in return for working at least twenty-two days a year. *Pas mal*, as they say in France.

David Blunkett, education secretary 1997–2001, home secretary 2001–2004, work and pensions secretary 2005

Three secretaryships for David Blunkett, once the local boss of what was known as the 'People's Republic of Sheffield', but not much to show for it. Was he unaware of all the possibilities on offer, or were his needs more modest than those of his colleagues? He's now an adviser on business development to A4e Ltd, for which he is entitled to be paid at least £25,000 a year, although (according to his parliamentary declaration of interests) he has not yet been paid. Perhaps he's waiting until he retires in 2015 and can go for the whole hog. A4e describes itself as a 'market leader in global public service reform', that is, privatization.

Lord Norman Warner, health minister 2003–2007

For a junior at the Health Ministry, Warner has done well, but let's not forget that he had special responsibility for 'reform' of the NHS – which meant overseeing greater private sector involvement. He met all the right people and in 2008, soon after Blair stepped down, Warner moved rapidly to a directorship with UK HealthGateway. He was also chairman of the Government Sector Advisory Panel for Xansa PLC – a leading provider of business outsource services to public bodies and holder of the £1 billion NHS shared business service centre contract, providing accounting and finance services to the NHS.

Not enough to keep him going? No. Warner became an adviser to Byotrol (a provider of micro-biological health treatments), Apax Partners Worldwide (a private equity firm with strong connections to the government which has invested heavily in health providers seeking contracts with the NHS), Deloitte (an accountancy and consultancy firm, with large incomes from government agencies) and DLA Piper (a legal firm, which, like Deloitte, specializes in advising on private contracting to the public sector).

Lord Warner remains influential within the NHS as chair of the NHS London Provider Agency. He was recently poached by Julian Le Grand (an LSE professor in social policy) on behalf of the Coalition government to help out on education in Birmingham. And why not? Revolving doors were installed for class war veterans like him.

Hilary Armstrong, secretary of state for local government 1997–2001, and for the cabinet office 2006–2007

Once regarded by some of Gordon Brown's partisans as rubbish, Hilary Armstrong has ignored her detractors and currently is chairperson of waste company SITA's advisory committee.

Nick Raynsford, local government and housing minister 1997–2005

Nick Raynsford is now non-executive chairman of local authority recruitment agency Rockpools PLC and of Home-track, a lettings service.

Ian McCartney, trade minister 1997–1999 and 2006–2007

McCartney was Number 10's weightiest link to the trade unions, briefing friendly journos on what was really going on. Now we all know. He is a senior adviser to the US Fluor Corporation, an energy contractor that is believed to have ambitions to win nuclear clean-up contracts in the UK. McCartney is paid at least £110,000 a year for his advice. The former Department of Trade and Industry had responsibility for energy policy.

Stephen Byers, trade and industry secretary 1998–2001

In contrast to his junior above, Stephen Byers, once a member of a far-left group, is now non-executive chairman of water treatment company ACWA and Ritz Climate Offset Company.

Richard Caborn, trade minister 1999–2001, sports minister 2001–2007

Richard Caborn, Yorkshire-born and Yorkshire-bred, used to boast he was a red – but he is now a consultant to AMEC assisting them with their work in the nuclear industry. His payment for this is at least £70,000 a year. As a former sports minister, he is also a consultant to the Fitness Industry Association, for which he is paid at least £10,000 a year. Small potatoes.

Brian Wilson, energy minister 2001–2003
Surprised that Brian Wilson is a non-executive director of AMEC Nuclear and UK chairman of the renewables company, Airtricity? Renewal, as some will recall, was a central theme of the Blair era.

Stephen Ladyman, transport minister 2005–2007
Stephen Ladyman is an adviser to Holdings, a company selling traffic information, for which he is paid at least £10,000 a year. Bravo, Stephen. Overpaid you're not.

Frank Field, welfare reform minister 1997–1998
Holier-than-thou Frank Field is now a director of Medicash, which, as its name suggests, operates a healthcare cash plan. Who better than fearless Frank to advise them?

Baroness Sally Morgan, in-house specialist
Sally Morgan was a very close and trusted aide of her dear leader, Tony Blair. As director of government relations in Downing Street she did not always endear herself to other colleagues, and perhaps for that reason was kicked upstairs to the House of Lords and made a minister. Her real career

blossomed: in November 2005 she was appointed as a non-executive director of the Carphone Warehouse Group. As well as being a non-executive director of TalkTalk from 2005 to 2010 and of Southern Cross Healthcare from 2006 to 2011, she sat on the LloydsPharmacy healthcare advisory panel. In April 2006 she became a board member of the Olympic Delivery Authority. She was appointed chair of Ofsted by the Conservative-led government from March 2011 but left in November 2014, after failing to be reappointed for a second three-year term.

A Dynamic Duo

Simon Stevens was Tony Blair's health adviser inside 10 Downing Street, and, with Alan Milburn, the key architect of the NHS privatization programme. Reward: chairman of UnitedHealth UK, which has won contracts with the NHS to manage and advise primary care trusts. The company's executive director, previously chief executive, was, until late 2007, Dr Richard Smith, a former editor of the *British Medical Journal*, currently working for UnitedHealth in the US. Darren Murphy was a special adviser to Prime Minister Blair from May 1997 to September 2005. After a period as head of government relations and external affairs for AstraZeneca UK, Murphy became managing director at the London office of lobbying firm APCO, whose clients include most of the private healthcare firms bidding to run Independent Sector Treatment Centres.

The NHS

The NHS, crippled by Blair and Brown with their PFIs and marketizations is now, thanks to this logic, well on its own way to total privatization, courtesy of the 2013 Health Act.[8] Youssef El-Ginghly, a Tower Hamlets GP, writing in the *Observer* in March 2013, described how the NHS is being dismantled and concluded:

> This is what saddens me: what were once the NHS's strengths – resources, expertise and the united focus on the patient – are being replaced by a fragmented and atomized service, bound not by a duty of care but by a

---

8   Max Pemberton wrote in the *Daily Telegraph* on 1 April 2013: 'Today is a landmark in the history of the NHS. I have no doubt that social historians will look back and define events in relation to this day; we will come to view things as pre- or post-April 1, 2013, in the same way that we currently think of before or after the establishment of the NHS.

'Today the Health and Social Care Act – in other words, the Coalition's highly controversial NHS reforms – comes into effect. So how will things change for those who rely on the NHS?

'It will not be obvious initially. People will get sick, see their GPs, be referred to specialists, be admitted to hospital or discharged, have blood tests and X-rays, and book appointments with physiotherapists and speech therapists, etc. There will be births and deaths. But, beneath the surface there will have been a dramatic shift in the way that healthcare is being delivered. Its impact should not be underestimated.'

contract and driven, not by what is best for the patient, but by the cost of the encounter. It will be a slow, insidious creep but it's coming. Be prepared. This is the way the NHS ends: not with a bang but a whimper.

As Allyson Pollock argues in the interview below, the only serious solution is for parliament to pass the NHS Reinstatement Bill, but this is not going to happen without mass protests supported by a large block of cross-party MPs who disrupt parliamentary business until the bill is passed. Given the composition of the extreme-centre parties, this seems unlikely.

The National Health Service and the Extreme Centre

An interview with Allyson Pollock, professor of public health research and policy at Queen Mary University of London

TARIQ ALI: How can the Health Service as it stands today resist the forward march of privatization?

ALLYSON POLLOCK: What is happening now in Europe is that we have got neoliberal policies coming from the US. The healthcare industry has exhausted the funds of America, where healthcare is running at about 18 per cent of GDP, compared with 9 or 10 per cent average in Europe. So the US healthcare investors need to find new markets, and they are busy attempting to penetrate and open up the healthcare systems of Europe. And of course the biggest trophy for them is the United Kingdom NHS, because it was for a long time the most socialized of all the healthcare systems.

So, since devolution, Scotland, Wales and England all have their own healthcare services. Scotland and Wales, which are very tiny, covering no more than eight or nine million people, have retained a national health service. But England, and many people don't realize this, abolished its national health service in 2012 with the Health and Social Care Act. What remains of the NHS is a funding stream, or a government pair, and the NHS has been reduced to a logo. The government is currently accelerating the break-up of what remains of the National Health Service under public ownership, closing hospitals, closing services, and privatizing or contracting out.

So just as we heard about how public lands in Liberia and Guinea are being transferred like enclosures to private owners from abroad, the same thing is happening with our public services. Our public hospitals, our public facilities are also being enclosed and given over to private-for-profit investors. And this is happening at an extraordinary speed in England. Faster than anywhere else in Europe. And this is a major global neoliberal project.

TA: To privatize health?

AP: Well, to privatize not just the healthcare system but also ultimately the funding. Now in the US, just under half of that

18 per cent of GDP is actually paid for by the government, but the government is in effect a taxpayer and then channels the money into private-for-profit corporations.

The government in England introduced the Health and Social Care Act because it wanted to open up new funding streams. It wants to reduce the level of services that are available publicly, create a climate of discontent with the NHS, forcing the middle classes to go private and pay either out of their pocket or with their healthcare insurance, so that we desert, we exit what is left.

But at the same time the government is reducing all our entitlements because there is no longer a duty to provide universal healthcare. That duty, that had been in place since 1948, was abolished in 2012. It means that now the government can reduce all the entitlements, reduce everything that is available, and increasingly we are going to have to pay personally or though private health insurance.

And the private health insurance industry is here. They have come here from the US and they are absolutely gearing up through the new structures the government has put in place to move into private-for-profit health insurance. And actually the new system the government is putting in place is modelled on the US. That will come at huge loss, and it will also be a public health catastrophe because it will mean that many, many millions will increasingly go without care, and of course markets render people invisible, they are not seen. The doctor in front of you only sees the patient that comes to him; he doesn't see the many tens of thousands who are being denied access to healthcare, which is why in the US the doctors are not out on the street campaigning.

But in the UK the doctors are out on the street campaigning, they are standing now for the National Health Alliance Party, they are putting in candidates to stand against the conventional parties. And so the doctors are still prepared to fight for universal healthcare. You have to use the parallel of the oak tree: it seems to be blooming and flourishing, but the roots have been severed and it can take many months or years for it to completely decay. And once it has gone, those doctors will no longer be there. They'll be like the doctors in the US, interested in themselves, interested in their own pockets and not interested in universal access to healthcare.

And this is the crime of the century, if you like, the way in which the English Coalition, both Conservative and Liberal Democrat, have actually abolished our NHS. But it should not be forgotten that they had a lot of help along the way from the Labour government before them.

TA: Labour set the basis for it when they were in power?

AP: Absolutely. Alan Milburn, the health secretary, did this in 2000. In 1997 the Labour government had its chance to reverse the privatization and marketization policies, to get rid of the Private Finance Initiative. And they had a very good secretary of state, Frank Dobson, who was quite determined to do some of that, but they got rid of him extra quick and instead we got Alan Milburn and his ten-year plan. And now he has gone off to join the very healthcare companies that he helped to build up.

That is the tragedy. When that bill was going through Parliament to abolish the NHS, many of the peers and many of the MPs had conflicts of interest. They actually had interests in the healthcare companies that they were establishing.

TA: It is outrageous, really. Just like the lawyer of the largest insurance company in the US who drafted the Obamacare Bill. And Alan Milburn is one of them!

AP: Yes, it's a travesty as far as democracy is concerned. It really is, and as a public health doctor it is an absolute catastrophe, because at the moment we know there are people of all ages with serious mental illnesses who cannot get access to healthcare; people with stroke, people with chronic illnesses, chronic diseases who are increasingly being denied access to healthcare. And they are voices in the wilderness, they are not being heard, because there is no collective mechanism for them to be heard any more.

And the doctors and nurses are absolutely in despair. Now we do have a solution: with my colleagues we've written an NHS Reinstatement Bill that we hope whichever party comes to power will actually run with so as to reinstate the NHS. There is a solution out there, drafted by people who know what needs to be done. It's written and ready.

TA: So now it's perfectly legitimate to make huge profits from the basic needs of ordinary people?

AP: Yes. From people's diseases and people's illnesses. Well, it began with the pharmaceutical industry and vaccine production. It is perfectly acceptable to make profits from vaccines, so why shouldn't we now go and make profits from illness and care? But of course the NHS in England was set up to be redistributive. It's funded through taxation, which is meant to be progressive, and the money is meant to flow according to need. But what we are now beginning to see is that money will flow according to the needs of shareholders and not patients, and that is a very real concern. Of course, it is all down to political will. Everything can be reversed but it comes down to politics, to democracy and to people making their voices heard.

The BBC

Apart from the NHS, the British institution that was once most greatly appreciated at home and admired abroad was the BBC, a model for similar outfits in Canada, Australia and India. Its radio broadcasts and, in the postwar period, television output were frequently ultra-deferential to monarch, prelate and prime minister, and this should not be forgotten. Simultaneously, however, the BBC hired independent-minded journalists and producers, many of whom shared a similar cultural, educational and class background to the upper echelons of the civil service and the bulk of the political elite, both Tory and Labour. The automated logic of the English class system undoubtedly worked through the BBC, but its director-generals (from founding father Lord Reith to the last of the mandarins, Alasdair Milne) were self-confident hierarchs, well aware that the institution could only work if producers were allowed to create an environment in which listeners and viewers could be properly informed, educated and entertained. If its credibility was seriously damaged, the edifice as a whole might be affected. Prior to the birth of television, the only filmed news was shown in cinema newsreels: Movietone, Gaumont, Paramount and in the dying days, Pathé(tic) kept moviegoers entertained by their patronizing simplicities. Even the better newsreels were thoroughly slavish. In 1932, as the National Hunger March Against the Means Test reached London, it was denounced by ministers as being inspired by Moscow. British Paramount News reported as follows:

And in Hyde Park, home of free speech, the marchers' leaders rally their followers with extremist speeches. The march is completely disorganized and the police are hard put to keep things moving. But the most humane force in the world has its own methods of keeping order. Mounted reinforcements are quickly on the scene.

Compared to this, it was not too difficult for BBC TV to present a more sophisticated face. This semi-independence was bolstered by the structure of the BBC, that conceptually resembled a duck-billed platypus: directly funded by the public via an annual licence fee collected by the government and handed over to the Corporation. Of course, the government had the power to raise the fee, and hence the facility to blackmail. It likewise appointed the board of governors who, in turn, selected the director-general or editor-in-chief of the BBC.

These heads were in most cases loyal to the system, but did not always equate this with servility to the political leaders of the day. There arose, as a result, frequent crises and clashes with politicians. In general, the Corporation functioned reasonably well and managed to defend its standards. Its controllers and other bosses tended to be men (yes, they were usually men) very different in character from the time-servers (frightened of their own shadows) and the over-employed caste of managers who determine the details of programming today.

Excerpts from the 1983 *Nationwide* interview that led to the end of live TV phone-ins involving the prime minister: Diana Gould, a Bristol housewife, questions Margaret Thatcher on the Falklands War.

BBC PRESENTER: For the next thirty-five minutes we will be inviting viewers around the country to put Mrs Thatcher on the spot, as we call it. We've been asking for questions over the last two weeks since the election was declared ... Let's go to Mrs Diana Gould in our Bristol studio. Mrs Gould, your question, please.

GOULD: Mrs Thatcher, why, when the *Belgrano*, the Argentinian battleship, was outside the exclusion zone and actually sailing away from the Falklands, why did you give the orders to sink it?

THATCHER: But it was not sailing away from the Falklands, it was in an area which was a danger to our ships and to our people on them.

GOULD: You have just said at the beginning of your answer that it was not sailing away from the Falklands, and I am asking you to correct that statement.

THATCHER: But it's within an area outside the exclusion zone, which I think is what you are saying is 'sailing away' ...

PRESENTER: I think we are not arguing about which way it was facing at the time.

THATCHER *(cross talk)*: ... which was a danger to our ships.

GOULD: Giving those orders to sink the *Belgrano* when it was actually sailing away from our fleet and away from the Falklands was, in effect sabotaging any possibility of any peace plans succeeding.

THATCHER: One day, all of the facts, in about thirty years' time, will be published.

GOULD: That is not good enough, Mrs Thatcher.

THATCHER: I am ... *(cross talk)* ... would you, please ... let me answer. Would you please let me answer. I think it could only be in Britain that a prime minister was accused of sinking an enemy ship that was a danger to our Navy, when my main motive was to protect the boys in our Navy.

Is the BBC in such a petrified or paralysed state today, so badly decayed, that it is beyond repair? Are all hopes of inner movement or structural reform misplaced? To read the national press this would appear to be the case. I'm not so sure. Hysteria reached absurd proportions in 2012 in the case of *Panorama* pulling a documentary on the dead entertainer Jimmy Savile, a serial child abuser as the whole of the country has since learned. The weak-kneed BBC senior man-agement found it difficult to explain themselves to a hostile public. Director-General George Entwistle, his predecessor Mark Thompson and Helen Boaden, director of news, were more reminiscent of mid-level bureaucrats in Honecker's East Germany than of creative-minded managers. Entwistle fell on his sword for a handsome pay-off. Others might have opted for hara-kiri.

There is an underlying problem that has confronted the BBC since Sir John Birt was made director-general in Thatcher's time. His predecessor but one had been sacked effectively on Thatcher's orders in 1987, for not 'being one of us'. A reliable toady, Marmaduke Hussey, was catapulted onto the BBC board as chairman. His first task was to sack Director-General Alasdair Milne for 'left-wing bias'. Thatcher was livid that the BBC had permitted her to be grilled on the Falklands War, live, by the articulate Mrs Gould from Bristol.

Thatcher disliked the BBC's coverage of the Falklands War and the miners' strike and highlighted a number of other documentaries that were considered 'too left-wing'. A faceless accountant, Michael Checkland, replaced Milne until the appointment of John Birt, a dalek-like figure without instincts or qualities, who transformed the BBC into the top-heavy managerial monster that it has become.

Birt anticipated that the Tories would privatize the BBC. He pre-empted this by institutionalizing private sector methods and dumbing down the BBC so effectively as to destroy any notion of diversity within British television. The number of managers assigned to broadcast units became a sad joke, and instead of considered argument, management-speak – lampooned fortnightly by *Private Eye* – became the norm. Not wishing to offend Thatcher, the BBC gave Murdoch much of what he wanted to stabilize Sky. Cricket, for instance, was no longer available to those who paid the licence fee.

When New Labour won, a New BBC was already in place. Blair and his principal spin doctors, Alastair Campbell and Peter Mandelson, turned out to be even bigger control freaks than Thatcher. Several senior BBC journalists and producers told me that government interference and bullying was qualitatively worse under Blair. Together with their pipsqueak subordinates, they regularly harassed producers complaining about what they perceived to be anti-government bias. Radio 4's *Today* programme became a favourite Blairite target. Simultaneously they were crawling to Murdoch at regular intervals, hobnobbing with the editors and staff of the *Sun* and happily inhaling the stench of the Murdoch stables.

After Birt's departure there was some improvement. Greg Dyke did have some instincts. For one he defended BBC journalists, for another he (sometimes) resisted the blandishments and abuse that emanated from Downing Street.

Just as the Falklands War had brought down Milne, the Iraq War did for Dyke. I have written about the BBC and Iraq at length elsewhere.[9] Outraged by an accurate report

---

9   Tariq Ali, *Rough Music: Blair/Bombs/Baghdad/London/ Terror* (London, 2005).

from Andrew Gilligan on the *Today* programme, based on
the views of a government scientist specializing in chemical
weapons, to the effect that the government had 'sexed up'
the evidence to go to war in Iraq, the Blair regime went into
action. Angry exchanges between Blair and Dyke followed.
On 18 July 2003, the scientist, Dr Kelly, was found dead
near his country home. Whether it was suicide (as in the
coroner's report) or murder remains the subject of debate.
Kelly's death shook Blair. Lord Hutton, a tame English judge
and a tried-and-tested servant of the state, was appointed
to head the inquiry. Dyke quoted the pollster Philip Gould,
an intellectually debased member of the Blair kitchen
cabinet, reassuring a nervous Labour peer: 'Don't worry, we
appointed the right judge.' Hutton ignored the bulk of the
evidence and declared the BBC guilty. Dyke had to resign,
while an exultant Alastair Campbell, crowing like a cock on
a dung heap, addressed the rest of the media. Hundreds of
BBC journalists assembled on the street to bid a fond fare-
well to Dyke. That, too, had never happened before.

The atmosphere of fear and the self-censorship that
followed are no secret. Under Birt, creativity had been suf-
focated. The new management structures had destroyed
departmental autonomy. Heads of departments no longer
had the same freedoms as before: current affairs, drama,
light entertainment all suffered. The right to fail, so essential to creativity, was no longer part of the deal. Ratings
and competition were all that mattered, give or take a
few good documentaries. It is hard to imagine a current

department boss taking on a contemporary equivalent of Monty Python, with the words: 'I don't like it myself, but make six programmes and then we'll see.' Ask those who work there.

This is the background to the present crisis. This is the reason why editors of TV programmes are too often scared to take the right decisions. This is why only yes-men are promoted. It is the culture of the BBC that needs to be over-hauled, its redundant parts (mainly brain-dead management appendages of various kinds) replaced and some freedom restored to programme-makers. There is no sign whatso-ever that this is what the extreme centre wants, and nothing will change unless there is an uprising by licence-fee payers.

2

Scottish Answers

Scotland has long been a nation. In September 2014, the Independence Referendum asked its citizens whether they now wished that nation to become a state. A majority replied in the negative, but within six weeks the polls revealed another shift: over 50 per cent of Scots now favoured independence. A campaign of fear accompanied by ideological tricks and tactical knavery had won the UK a victory, but it is unlikely to be permanent. As Neil Davidson wrote in the *New Left Review*, too much has changed to move backwards again:

> By the time the electoral rolls closed on 2 September 2014, some 97 per cent of the Scottish population had registered to vote: 4,285,323 people, including 109,000 of the sixteen- and

seventeen-year-olds specially enfranchised for the occasion. This was the highest level of voter registration in Scottish or British history since the introduction of universal suffrage. By the time the ballot closed at 10pm on 18 September, 3,619,915 had actually voted, an 85 per cent turnout, compared with 65 per cent in the 2010 British general election. The popular vote was 2,001,926 for No, 1,617,989 for Yes, or 55 to 45 per cent against Scotland becoming an independent country. The demographics were telling. The No vote was heavily weighted towards the elderly: a clear majority of over-fifty-fives voted No, including nearly three-quarters of over-sixty-fives, many giving pensions or fears about savings and the currency as the main reason. Women were slightly more inclined to vote No than men, though that may partly reflect female predominance in the older age groups. Among under-forties there was a clear majority for Yes, with the strongest showing among twenty-five- to thirty-four-year-olds, 59 per cent of whom voted for independence. Based on pre-referendum polling, a significant majority of Scots of Asian origin voted Yes. In general, the No vote was correlated with higher income and class status; in the poorest neighbourhoods and peripheral housing schemes, the Yes vote was 65 per cent; it was from this group that most of the new voters emerged. One striking feature was the clash between the referendum results and regional party loyalties. The working-class Yes vote was concentrated in what were formerly the great heartlands of Labour support, above all in Dundee (57 per cent Yes) and Glasgow (54 per cent Yes), with similar results in North Lanarkshire and West Dumbartonshire;

Inverclyde came within eighty-eight votes of a Yes majority. On the other hand, Aberdeenshire, 'Scotland's Texas' and an SNP stronghold which includes Salmond's Holyrood constituency, voted against independence.[1]

It was intellectually exhilarating, during two trips to Scotland over the summer of 2014, to witness and participate in the serious debates taking place in meeting halls, kirks, streets, pubs and homes. What a contrast to dreary old England, where all three parties and every single media outlet were against Scottish independence! The No campaign lacked both sense and subtlety, being based exclusively on fear.

In contrast, the SNP, and even more the Radical Independence Campaign, looked at a detached Scotland through international spectacles. Their gaze was fixed on the Norwegian model and beyond. A few months ago, in an open letter to the people of Scotland published by the *Herald*, some of Scandinavia's leading writers and intellectuals encouraged the birth of an independent state, reminding Scots that Norway's break from Sweden in 1905 was also preceded by fear-mongering – and yet it improved the quality of life and politics in both countries.

The remarkable growth in the pro-independence movement is the result of long-term causes: Thatcher's dismantling of the welfare state and Blair–Brown's

---

1   Neil Davidson, 'A Scottish Watershed', *New Left Review*, September–October 2014.

embrace of the same process. Until then, the Scots had been prepared to stick to Labour regardless of the corruption and chicanery that categorized its party machine in Scotland. When large numbers stop believing that they can exercise political self-determination within the existing social order, they begin to look beyond traditional governing parties. On the Continent (and in England) this has led to the growth of the right. In Scotland what was on offer was national, social and political self-determination.

Why did this happen, and what will be its impact within the United Kingdom and the larger European community? How is it that so many Scottish people now feel that only through independence can Scotland realize its full political and cultural potential in the twenty-first century?

Scotland was tricked into the Union with England in 1707. Sold down the river, many of its poets thought. Robert Burns, probably the greatest of all Scottish poets, summed it up in a famous song:

> What force or guile could not subdue,
> Thro' many warlike ages,
> Is wrought now by a coward few,
> For hireling traitor's wages.
> The English steel we could disdain,
> Secure in valour's station;
> But English gold has been our bane –
> Such a parcel of rogues in a nation!

Burns was making the point that it was easy to buy off the nobility with a bit of lucre and some promises. The Scottish aristocrats effectively capitulated to the Union. And Sir Walter Scott has an equally pithy comment on what then happened: 'It may be doubted whether the descendants of the noble lords who accepted this gratification would be more shocked at the general fact of their ancestors being corrupted or scandalized by the paltry amount of the bribe.'

And for a long time this Union has flourished.

The weakness in traditional Scottish nationalism lay in its inability to grasp that identity could not be the only factor in the march to independence. As Tom Nairn and numerous other Scottish intellectuals have pointed out, the Union was a compact between the English bourgeoisie and a weak and desperate Scottish elite, one of whose rewards was entry into English markets and later access to its colonies in North America and Asia. Five of the British viceroys who ruled India were members of the Scottish gentry. Scottish administrators were a cornerstone of the imperial bureaucracies in Asia and Africa.

For the latter half of the nineteenth century and the first half of the twentieth, the Scottish elites benefited greatly; the subaltern layers less so. As a proportion of population, Scottish deaths exceeded English ones in the First World War. There were other downsides as well. Scotland's political identity was destroyed; a massive emigration to North America, and secondarily to Australia, followed the brutal Highland Clearances. The emigrants were not just the remnants of the defeated clans, but included every layer of Scottish society. The reasons were not only economic: many Scots turned their back on a country occupied by the English redcoats.

Two processes combined to reawaken Scotland. The depression of the thirties left a deep mark on the country, and the end of empire a decade later, after yet another war, created the basis for new thinking. The Labour Party itself, born in Scotland and the product of many Scottish politicians and trade unions and workers, had been pledged to Scottish home rule. But after Labour won its landslide victory in 1945, Clement Attlee introduced welcome reforms which included free education, a health service free at the point of delivery for every citizen in the country, and subsidized house-building, enabling people to live in sometimes ugly but still better buildings than before. This desire to improve living standards won over Scotland wholesale to Labour, and discussion of independence became muted.

The new nationalist turn was the result of a democratic deficit. After 1979, the bulk of Scotland voted against Margaret Thatcher three times, and came to feel that they were no longer represented in the English Parliament. Often when one visited Scotland in those days people would say it was 'none of our business, we voted against the Tories …' And it was this that shook the Union's foundations.

Initially there were hopes that Labour would be different. But when Tony Blair followed suit, emulating Thatcher and reducing the Scottish Parliament to little more than a local council, the haemorrhage of Labour votes began. Labour's more enlightened leaders on this question, John Smith and Donald Dewar, both important politicians in Scotland, had assumed that devolution would solve the problem.

But devolution did not give the Scottish Parliament the right to levy taxes. Amid mounting demands for wider parliamentary powers, the Scottish Nationalist Party came to the fore, arguing effectively for a social democratic Scotland rather than a Thatcherite, conservative Scotland. The irony was that while the Scottish Tories, or Conservatives and Unionists as they called themselves, were more or less wiped out at this time, their place was taken in Scotland by New Labour, to which all that mattered was money, and what happened in the City of London was much more important than anything going on in Scotland.

Small wonder that support for independence was strongest among working people. The notion that an independent Scotland would be parochial was not taken seriously by anyone inside Scotland itself. The so-called internationalism of New Labour and its Coalition lookalikes was limited to subordinating the entire British polity to the interests of the United States. They made the United Kingdom a vassal state as regards decisions towards Iraq and Afghanistan, even as regards the gathering of intelligence. In response it was felt that an independent Scotland could be far more internationalist and autonomous, and might benefit a great deal from links to both Scandinavia and states in other continents.

What happened then was that a campaign of fear began. And this campaign of fear succeeded. Here there are many parallels with another part of Europe: the way the European elites had treated Greece when there was a danger that the radical party Syriza might win the last general election.

Every single European head of state who mattered, the German, the French, the British establishments began pleading with the Greek people: don't vote Syriza, if you vote Syriza your pensions will disappear. If you vote Syriza there will be no medicines in the shops, you will die; everything will collapse. Well, lots of Greeks knew that everything had already collapsed after what they had been subjected to by the Troika. But the elderly and the pensioners were scared enough to accept this propaganda, and Syriza lost by a small margin.

All the same, the party is now way ahead of all its rivals and were an election to be held tomorrow, it would win, forming the largest party in the Greek parliament. People have realized they were tricked. In Britain, a similar campaign was waged by all three Unionist parties – Labour, Tory and Liberal Democrats – supported by a few misguided individuals and media on the left, including pathetic hangers-on like George Galloway, the left-wing Respect MP for Bradford West, trying to curry favour with his former party bosses.

During three visits to Scotland in the summer leading up to the referendum, I witnessed a society that, unlike its southern big brother, was very much alive. The extreme-centre parties, openly collaborating to prevent independence, waged a 'Better Together' campaign which lacked any sense of subtlety. They offered little that was positive. Their arguments, as had been predicted by many, were based exclusively on fear. These were the forces of pessimistic conservatism in Scotland. These were the people who appeared shallow and parochial.

How many times did I hear people say in Scotland, 'We never realized how important we were ... to ourselves'? People told me how there had been no community spirit left in many parts of the big cities like Glasgow and Edinburgh – 'and we suddenly found ourselves talking to each other again, debating with our neighbours, debates taking place in each household and this made us believe in ourselves.' This has been the most important aspect of the campaign in Scotland: a mass revival of politics.

And this mass interest in politics was noticed by everyone, even visiting commentators from metropolitan London. They found the Yes camp had reignited politics. Why? Because people felt that if they moved off their backsides and went and campaigned and agitated and struggled they could bring about change. Elsewhere in the Continent, as in England, these activities have fuelled a shift to the right. What was being offered in Scotland opened up new opportunities for self-organization, and the campaign was totally political. Moreover the SNP was extremely intelligent in its approach, not pandering to the stereotypes which the English, few of whom know Scotland, are conditioned to expect.

The last-minute panic of the extreme centre was pathetic, grotesque to behold. Politicians who had never even visited Scotland suddenly poured in. Sixty MPs on one day were scrambled by train northwards. It was obvious that the metropolitan elite was totally out of touch. Having not taken the campaign too seriously, supremely confident that they were going to sweep through, they belatedly realized that the contest was getting closer and closer.

Remarkably, even in the tiniest communities in the North – the Shetland Islands, the Outer Hebrides – people were asking themselves, 'Do we want to be part of an independent nation?' And many, many were surprised at the scale of the majority in these regions voting Yes. The same went for the cities. An opinion poll in the last days of the campaign, which stunned the No camp, revealed that Glasgow was going for independence, and this meant that the Labour Party, which had ruled parts of Scotland for a long time, was losing its grip.

So how was this greeted by the media? Here we have a

very interesting comparison with what happened in Latin America. Throughout the emergence of the Bolivarians – the social movements against privatization and for a new way of life – 99 per cent of the media in Venezuela, the media in Bolivia, the media in Ecuador, opposed the new aspirations and campaigned viciously and brutally against the Bolivarians; but still they won.

Here, the Unionist left and the Unionist right combined to attack any notion of Scottish independence. Will Hutton wrote in the *Observer*: 'If Britain can't find a way of sticking together, it is the death of the liberal enlightenment before the atavistic forces of nationalism and ethnicity – a dark omen for the twenty-first century. Britain will cease as an idea. We will all be diminished.' Talk like that actually reminds one of the language bandied about at the peak of the British Empire. The break-up of Britain might well diminish people like Will Hutton and his ilk; others might see it as an opportunity to bring about a few changes here.

In contrast, George Monbiot of the *Guardian* delivered a very fine column two days before the vote. 'No United Kingdom newspaper', he wrote, 'except the *Sunday Herald* supports Scottish independence.' He then quoted Melanie Reid in *The Times*: 'What spoilt, selfish, childlike fools these Scots are. They simply don't have a clue how lucky they are.' In a similar vein, in the *Spectator* Simon Heffer maintained that 'addicted to welfare, Scots embraced the something-for-nothing society, objecting to the Poll Tax because many of them felt that paying taxes ought to be the responsibility of someone else.'

Things also got personal. As Monbiot commented, 'Here is the chronic inability to distinguish between a cause and a person. The referendum is widely portrayed as a vote about Alex Salmond, who is then monstered beyond recognition.' A *Telegraph* editorial compared Salmond to Robert Mugabe, while the *Daily Express* referred to him as a 'dictator'.

Such attitudes were not only carried in the corporate press, owned by mighty barons such as Rupert Murdoch or the Barclay twins, or in the tabloids of certain former porn merchants and other worthies (and as for the wealthy Russian proprietors of the *Independent*, they were all for maintaining the Union). What would the *Guardian* do? A newspaper not owned by anyone except the Trust, it too was caught up in the tidal wave of Unionist reaction. Its editorials effectively defended the Union, and while it gave some space to opposition voices its own in-house columnists, with the exception of Monbiot, were all singing different lines from the Unionist hymn sheet. Seumas Milne attacked Alex Salmond as effectively a Tartan Tory, ignoring what Scottish Labour had done to that country and the reasons why so many Labour Party supporters were joining the SNP. Young Owen Jones wrote in a similar vein, but more open-mindedly than Milne. Steve Bell, one of the most brilliant cartoonists in Europe, usually on the right side, was also infected by the

Unionist fervour, portraying Alex Salmond as tucked in Murdoch's pocket.[2]

Thus it was despite the media that the Scottish movement – a political uprising for creating a Scotland with a proper health service, a free education system and more social housing – soldiered on and almost won the battle. Had it done so, it would have been catastrophic for the British state.

The vote in Scotland was close. The No's narrowly squeezed through, but even those who support them know full well that the process will not end there. They have been promised, not bags of gold as their predecessors were in 1707, but something called 'Devo Max'.

In other words, in order to win, the extreme centre promised that the Scottish Parliament would be allowed to determine practically everything related to Scotland, apart from defence or foreign policy. But this, of course, will only halt the tide temporarily. I think the movement is now so far advanced that if the Scots continue to feel dissatisfied, which I'm sure they will, in a few years' time there will be a huge demand for another referendum. And this time they will make it.

---

2   Add to this the maverick figure of George Galloway. He, too, took great delight in sharing platforms with 'Better Together' worthies and was often more virulent than them in attacking the Yes camp. Small wonder the home secretary, Theresa May, tweeted: 'Good for George Galloway. The only man giving voice to those who believe in the Union.'

In the meantime, the voting figures revealed the extent to which working-class strongholds had opted for independence: 53.49 per cent voted Yes in Glasgow, 57.3 per cent voted Yes in Dundee. In the weeks following the victory of the UK there was an astonishing influx of new members to the SNP, and also to the Greens. The former catapulted from 25,642 to 68,200 members, while the latter trebled from 1,720 to 6,235. In polar contrast, Scottish Labour was in meltdown. Its ineffective and wooden leader, Johann Lamont, resigned in a huff, accusing Westminster and Ed Miliband of controlling every tiny tactic in the campaign. As if to push the knife in further, opinion polls in Scotland revealed that if the vote was held today (October 2014) 52 per cent would vote for separation. Rarely has a nation rejected the outcome of its own poll so rapidly.

The cliffhanger now is how Scotland will vote in the 2015 general election. If the 'Better Together' parties, principally Labour, get a severe beating and the SNP doubles or trebles its MPs in Westminster, the game will be nearly over. Scottish independence will become a question of timing. In 2016 there will be new elections to the Scottish Parliament. These will be an important test. If, as is widely predicted, the pro-independence parties get a large majority, a new debate will begin in earnest, centring on the future of Scotland. What numerous pundits in the media have not understood is that many in Scotland want self-determination not because they are anti-English, but because they are deeply hostile to the Thatcher–Blair consensus that still rules England, regardless of party.

On a single day in Glasgow, a murky Saturday in November 2014, 13,000 people came to a political rally to hear the new SNP leader, Nicola Sturgeon, outline her programme, breaking into thunderous applause when she insisted that Scotland would get rid of the nuclear weapons stationed on its soil. The SNP conference rejected a call for an Alliance for Independence as an umbrella to contest the Westminster elections. Unwise, in my opinion; but they did open the door to people from different traditions and roots where it was clear they commanded popular support. In this case they could stand under the SNP banner. Some will. Others will wait for better times. There is a strong feeling that the unity of the forces that want independence must not be broken.

A few hundred yards away the Radical Independence Campaign, attended by over 3,000 people, was discussing in a sober and mature fashion the future of their country. One of their mass forums was attended by representatives from Quebec, Spanish Podemos and Greek Syriza, bringing messages of support from their respective movements.

I have never experienced an event like this anywhere in Britain over the last fifty years. Of course there have been huge demonstrations, strikes and suchlike. This was something different. A new politics of the left was being created, a politics which, of necessity, will soon, I hope, be represented in the Scottish Parliament. The debate on how Scottish space should be reorganized will be held in public view. The Scottish writer, Alan Bissett, presented the People's Vow to conclude the conference, prefacing it thus: 'As democrats, we recognize the result of the referendum but acknowledge the collusion, from all corners of the British establishment, to deceive and intimidate the Scottish electorate into voting in a way which maintained their right to rule. It was ever thus, but not how it need remain.'

Nothing remotely like this exists in England. Here right-wing Tories can defect to Ukip, but not one of the four or five left-wing MPs in the Parliamentary Labour Party would even consider such a prospect. In fact England, too, needs a People's Vow. To campaign for similar policies and challenge the extreme centre and the sprouting New Right. Clinging to the fraying coattails of the 'labour movement' is a recipe for inaction. Politics, not sociology, is the need of the decade.

The People's Vow

1. We won't let the poor suffer any longer for errors made by bankers and politicians. Our movement will endorse higher wages and deeper investment over greed and the backslapping bonus culture. Social justice campaigners everywhere, whether in Edinburgh, London, Cardiff, Dublin or Barcelona, can expect our full support because our challenges are international. Together with trade unions, community groups, charities and academic experts, we will prepare a people's budget to save Scottish public services.

2. We won't let anyone sell our natural resources to the highest bidder. Scotland has a unique physical inheritance, and polluters are not welcome to it because it belongs to us. We will make sure the Scottish government uses planning laws to stop fracking, and we will support direct action against fracking companies if they continue to threaten our environment. Green energy is the only civilized future, and we promise to make Scotland a model country for the twenty-first century by combining social and environmental justice.

3. Scotland's feudal legacy will end. We won't allow the next Holyrood government to leave communities at the mercy of corrupt landlords. Scotland's people will have the power to own and control their resources. Our land will support our goals of sustainability and social justice: it won't be used as hunting and fishing estates for aristocrats and tax exiles. We will call a demonstration for land reform centred in one of Scotland's rural communities.

4. We won't allow equality to become a buzzword. We will expect positive action to reverse inequalities between men and women, and we will punish politicians who fail to take this seriously. Our better Scotland must abandon the macho political culture of Westminster and the macho economic culture of the City of London. We pledge to make our company boards, QUANGOs and political parties representative of Scotland as a whole. Fifty-fifty representation for men and women is a minimum; we'll make equality compulsory, not an afterthought left to the whims of employers.

5. We won't let NATO use Scotland as a dumping ground for nuclear weapons. If politicians fail to act in 2015, we will launch an intensive campaign of civil disobedience against Trident to highlight the deep inequalities between public opinion and Westminster. Nor will we tolerate laws that put our vital public services in peril to global corporations. TTIP is wrong for Scotland just as it is wrong for working people on both sides of the Atlantic. We pledge our opposition to TTIP in Scotland. Scotland's National Health Service will remain in public hands, where it should be.

3

The Corbyn Factor

Pundits on Parade

Wrong, wrong and wrong again. Was ever there a more crassly inept politician than Jeremy Corbyn, whose every impulse is to make the wrong call on everything? ... May can only gain a two-thirds majority in the Commons if Labour agrees to its own annihilation – which he welcomes. Will this be the last disastrous disservice he does to his party?

Polly Toynbee, *Guardian*, 19 April

Theresa May was trounced and 'Jez we can' was no wishful fantasy ... What hubris of May to call an election in the face of the longest, most sustained wage-fall in living memory.

– Polly Toynbee, *Guardian*, 9 June

By any standards it is an extraordinary document. Detailed, deadly serious, utterly candid and unashamedly moral, the Tories' 84-page manifesto yesterday unveiled Mayism (a word she hates) and British politics entered a new era. Gone were the gimmicks, glitz and disingenuity of the Cameron and Blair eras, and the cynical manifestos replete with pledges their authors had no intention of keeping. Nor did Theresa May try to exploit her opponents' weakness by playing safe. Instead, with a clear ethical – even Christian – tone, this vicar's daughter took the riskier option: to be unremittingly honest with the public about the great challenges this country faces, to spell out how she intends to confront them and to promise only what she can deliver. This was a grown-up politician treating the electorate as grown-ups.

– *Daily Mail* editorial, 19 May

As for why the Conservatives' commanding lead all but evaporated, the reasons are not hard to find. The party went to the country on a deeply flawed manifesto, drawn up by a tiny clique of advisers at No 10, committed to such vote-losing policies as a free Commons vote on foxhunting and means-testing pensioners' winter fuel allowance.

– *Daily Mail* editorial, 10 June

～

One thing is certain: this is going to be a very bad election for a divided Labour party and a weak Jeremy Corbyn.

– Sebastian Payne, *Financial Times*, 18 April

I never thought that I would feel sorry for Jeremy Corbyn, but today I do.

> – Matthew d'Ancona, *Guardian*, 18 April

It is a bold decision and one that affords Mrs May the opportunity to become as dominant a figure on the political stage as Margaret Thatcher was 30 years ago … she is right to call an election.

> – *Daily Telegraph* editorial, 18 April

In terms of share of the vote, Labour's result in June will draw comparisons with Michael Foot's disastrous campaign against Margaret Thatcher in 1983.

> – Former Labour MP Tom Harris, *Daily Telegraph*, 19 April

My own view is that despite the twists and turns of this increasingly surreal campaign, Corbyn will struggle to significantly exceed the 31 per cent Ed Miliband achieved in 2015, while Theresa May is locked in with about 45 per cent of the vote. Anything less than a Conservative majority in excess of 100 seats would be surprising.

> – Dan Hodges, *Mail on Sunday*, 4 June

General Election Seat by Seat: My final predictions – A Tory Landslide is Still On.

> – Iain Dale, iaindale.com, 5 June

~

Mrs May isn't just kicking Corbyn when he's down, she's dug his political grave, prepared the coffin, set the date for the funeral service and invited us all to attend his career death ... if Corbyn leads Labour into this General Election on 8 June, I fear he's going to get beaten so badly the party itself may never recover and Britain will move forward with no viable opposition party.

– Piers Morgan, *Mail Online*, 18 April

As exit poll looms, I repeat my prediction: Conservatives to win by 90–100 seat majority.

– Piers Morgan, Twitter, 8 June

Mr Corbyn has proved a lot of people, including me, completely wrong.

– Piers Morgan, Twitter, 9 June

~

Let me be the first to say, I got it wrong, wholly wrong.

– Iain Dale, LBC, 9 June

I was wrong about Jeremy Corbyn.

– John Rentoul, *Independent*, 9 June

I wasn't a bit wrong, or slightly wrong, or mostly wrong, but totally wrong.

– Owen Jones, *Guardian*, 9 June

Good evening. I know nothing. We, the media, the experts, the pundits, know nothing.

— Jon Snow, *Channel 4 News*, 9 June

I was wrong.

— Jonathan Freedland, *Guardian*, 10 June

Here, I consume a monster helping of humble pie ... I was wrong.

— Andrew Rawnsley, *Observer*, 11 June

I was wrong.

— Nick Cohen, *Observer*, 11 June

As I was saying last week, or at least as the headline on this column accurately summed it up: 'Don't panic ... May is well ahead.' Wrong, Lawson, and not for the first time in this campaign.

— Dominic Lawson, *Sunday Times*, 11 June

We all got it wrong.

— Jess Phillips, *Observer*, 11 June

(Quotes courtesy of *Private Eye*, Election Special, Issue 1446)

On 18 April 2017, the Conservative prime minister, Theresa May, alongside her principal political adviser, Nick Timothy, presided over a supine cabinet. Unexpectedly, she cut short the life of her government, which had three years still to run, triggering a six-week period leading up to a general election on 8 June.

The motives were obvious. Since 2010 David Cameron's government – backed by Blairite Labour and the Liberal Democrats – had proceeded smoothly enough until it sailed headlong into a storm and foundered on the hard rock of Brexit. Every single party in parliament on 23 June 2016 had voted to Remain. In contrast, the majority of the country voted to Leave. It was, as I suggested at the time, a scream of rage against neoliberalism and the politics of the extreme centre. Cameron immediately resigned as prime minister, and Theresa May was immediately ushered into 10 Downing Street as a compromise replacement. Ten months later, with Labour trailing twenty points, she thought the future belonged to her. So did the media and a bulk of the excremental Parliamentary Labour Party.

What did she want as she called the snap election? For starters a much larger majority, preferably sixty to seventy more MPs in the House of Commons to strengthen her own position vis-à-vis Labour and the SNP. Secondly, to give herself a free hand within the Conservative Party so that she and her advisers could handle the Brexit negotiations as they wished. Finally, to destroy Corbyn and his unruly cohort.

However, on 8 June, the Conservatives said goodbye to their majority in parliament, losing safe seats in Canterbury and Kensington to a Corbyn-led Labour

Party. In contrast, Labour obtained its second-highest popular vote since the party was founded. How did this come to pass?

It had been assumed she would win a huge majority, since Jeremy Corbyn was regarded as an extremely weak opponent. It didn't turn out quite like that, posing a serious question to all those who got it so badly wrong. How did a political party, brutally written off by the media–extreme centre nexus, campaigning on behalf of a suffering and aggrieved public crushed by one humiliation after another, organize a fightback that came close to victory? And this despite the brazen distortions and lies emanating daily from the state broadcaster and the print media, as exemplified by the petty, spiteful and malicious material circulated by the *Guardian* since Corbyn's election as party leader in 2015. Small wonder that large numbers of people, especially the young, stopped reading newspapers or believing the BBC, and sought their news elsewhere.

Labour did not win, but Theresa May lost her majority. She was forced to rely on the parliamentarians belonging to a somewhat deranged party of the Ulster fundamentalist right. Her project lay in ruins. The extreme centre has been dented.

This story, however, began two years earlier.

In 2015, the UK state – its economy, its culture, its fractured identities and party system – was in a much deeper crisis than many wanted to accept. Its governors, at least in public, were in semi-denial. English politicians assumed that the threat to the unitary state had been seen off after they got the result they wanted in the Scottish independence referendum. The results of the 2015 general election appeared to suggest otherwise. The Scottish National Party (SNP) exercised a virtual monopoly of Scottish representation in the House of Commons and one opinion poll indicated a small majority in favour of Scottish independence.

The impact of this on the crisis of Labourism, old and new, should not be underestimated. It is the most dramatic change in the UK party system since the foundation of the Labour Party itself. Within Labour Ed Miliband resigned as leader following the defeat. The caretaker leader, Harriet Harman, then decided not to oppose the Tories on the basic tenets of their austerity policies: she knew that a post-2015 Labour government would have done the same. The party that lost the election was conformist and visionless: it had forgotten what it meant to mount an opposition. Could they recover?

Add to all this the following facts: 11.3 million votes obtained 331 seats for the Conservatives; 9.3 million got Labour 232 MPs; the Liberal Democrats with 2.4 million went down to eight; while the Greens and Ukip gained a single MP each for a million plus and 3.8 million votes respectively. A blatantly rigged electoral mechanism is not a cause for celebration; whatever else it may be, this is clearly not a representative democracy.

The slowly deteriorating situation in the UK had been masked for decades by euphoria engendered by the huge triumph of capitalism. Since the nineties, easy credit helped create a sea of household debt in the US and UK, the scale and size of which was unprecedented. Small wonder that politicians and bankers became giddy with success. Politics had become little more than concentrated neoliberal economics, and a faulty version at that. The speculative excess of the late 1990s ended with the dot-com bubble, while the financial earthquake of 2008 shook capitalism to its core, without actually destroying it, thanks to state intervention.

Nonetheless, after every setback, the bankers and the politicians decided to carry on in the same way: helping themselves to shocking amounts of public money. A few of neoliberalism's architects – economists rather than politicians – lost the faith. At least partially. The joys of globalization were forgotten as the preachers of austerity took to their pulpits and pleaded with the poor to become poorer. A couple of columnists in the *Financial Times*, once ardent champions of the new order, decided that a carefully organized retreat was necessary to shore up the system and prevent upheavals ('populism') from below. Something had to be done.

A move from monetary policy to a fiscal regime was necessary to rebuild a more shockproof version of the system: capitalism with a human face. This view, by no means universal, was nonetheless accepted by an influential minority of US economists and by more than a few of their British peers attached to the Bank of England.

The mainstream politicians were happy to follow in tow rather than lead. For most of them the modern variant of capitalism had acquired the aura of a mystical religion in which the financial speculator was the key producer of economic values. Unsurprisingly, the link between the money men and centre politicians of every hue became ever closer. Could anything animate the frozen night of English politics? And where might the first signs of spring appear?

The new system for Labour leadership elections introduced by Ed Miliband in 2014 was meant as a conciliatory gesture. He had been accused of only winning the leadership with the support of the hated trade unions, so he instituted a one-member, one-vote system for every party member or supporter who was prepared to part with £3. It was a step forward for democratization, which had the overwhelming support of the Parliamentary Labour Party (PLP). Most of them assumed that if outsiders had any effect at all it would help seal the status quo.

And so it might have been had New Labour managed to come up with a halfway credible candidate, but talent in these quarters was in very short supply. None of the mainstream candidates, male or female, fitted the bill. Their politics were barely different from the Tories'. Their desire to keep the bankers happy was coupled with an inability to understand that occasionally some things have to be changed in order for everything that matters to remain the same. In order to preserve the fiction that the PLP remained a broad church that favoured diversity and loved a good debate, a few Blairites gave their vote to support a candidate from the minuscule parliamentary left. This strategy had worked before: last time around David Miliband had patronisingly nominated Diane Abbott as a candidate. In 2015 the hardcore right hoped a left candidate might take away support from Andy Burnham, who was what passed for leftish and hence not fully trustworthy. This would leave the door open for the centrists' candidates Liz Kendall or Yvette Cooper to fight it out without hindrance.

Enter Jeremy Corbyn, stage left. He may not be as charismatic a figure as his late mentor Tony Benn, but nor could he ever be mistaken for a PR confection. I have shared numerous platforms with him over the past forty years and on all key issues he has remained steadfast. During the leadership debates he came across as uninterested in point-scoring and oblivious to media hostility. He criticized the doctrine of privatization and denounced the pro-war foreign policy of all recent governments.

During the contest the *Guardian* came out for Yvette Cooper, the *Mirror* for Andy Burnham. Absolutely nobody, including Corbyn himself, thought that he could win. The campaign was intended just to show that there was an alternative to the neoliberal leadership that had ruled the country for the last three decades. However, what appealed to the young and to the many who had left the party in disgust during the Blair–Brown years was precisely what alienated the political and media cliques. They, in turn, turned a leadership contest into a social movement.

Corbyn was untutored, discursive, too left-wing and wanted to reverse the privatizations of the railways and utilities, end tuition fees and cancel Trident. Many who joined the Labour Party after its electoral defeat did so to break from the bland, unimaginative, conformist and visionless politics of New Labour, an outfit that had forgotten what it meant to be an opposition party. All Corbyn's opponents were more or less in favour of Osborne's austerity measures and his predecessor, Ed Miliband, had voted in favour of ending tax credits, the mildest of ameliorative measures borrowed by Brown from Bill Clinton's White House.

Corbyn's campaign generated a mass movement that renewed the base of the Labour Party – nearly 250,000 new members and counting – and led to his triumph. He won almost as many votes as all his opponents put together. Blair's misjudged appeals ('Hate me as much as you want, but don't vote Corbyn') and Brown's out-of-touch attacks accusing Corbyn of being friendly with dictatorships (he was referring to Venezuela, rather than Saudi Arabia or Kazakhstan, states favoured by the New Labour elite) only won Corbyn more support. The Blairite cohort that dominates the *Guardian*'s opinion pages – Jonathan Freedland, Polly Toynbee et al. – had zero impact on the result, keen though they were to trash Corbyn. They were desperate enough even to give space – twice – to Blair himself, in the hope of rehabilitating him. Naturally, the paper lost many readers, including me.

Corbyn's victory was not based on ultra-leftism. His views reflected what many in the country felt, and this is what anti-Corbyn Labour found difficult to grasp. The candidate spelled it out himself in one of the TV debates:

> We also as a party have to face up to something which is an unpleasant truth, that we fought the 2015 election on very good policies included in the manifesto but fundamentally we were going to be making continuing cuts in central government expenditure, we were going to continue underfunding local government, there were still going to be job losses, there were still going to be people suffering because of the cuts we were going to impose by accepting an arbitrary date to move into budget surplus, accepting the language of austerity. My suggestion is that the party has to challenge the politics of austerity, the politics of increasing the gap between the richest and the poorest in society and be prepared to invest in a growing economy rather than accepting what is being foisted on us by the banking crisis of 2008 to 2009. We don't have to set this arbitrary date, which in effect means the poorest and most vulnerable in our society pay for the banking crisis rather than those that caused it.

How could any Labour MP disagree with that?

What they really hated was his questioning of the private sector. John Prescott had been allowed to pledge the renationalization of the railways at the 1996 Labour Party Conference, but after Blair's victory the following year the subject was never raised again. Until now.

When I asked him when he first realized he might actually win, Corbyn's response was characteristic of the activist that he remains: 'It was in Nottingham during the last weeks of campaigning ... Normally we think that fifty or sixty people at a meeting is a good turnout. I got four hundred and there were people outside who couldn't get in. I thought then we might win this one.' The crowds grew and grew, making clear that Corbyn was capable of mobilizing and inspiring large numbers of people, and making clear too how flimsy the support was, outside the media, for the other candidates.

His election animated English politics. His horrified enemies in the PLP immediately started to plot his removal. Lord Mandelson informed us that the PLP wouldn't destroy their new leader immediately: 'It would be wrong', he wrote, 'to try and force this issue from within before the public have moved to a clear verdict.' Blair, angered by this outburst of democracy in a party that he had moulded in his own image, declared that the Labour Party would be unelectable unless Corbyn was removed. Brown kept relatively quiet, perhaps because he was busy negotiating his very own private finance initiative with the investment firm Pimco (Ben Bernanke and the former ECB president Jean-Claude Trichet are also joining its 'global advisory board').

The establishment decided to wheel out the chief of defence staff, Sir Nicholas Houghton. Interviewed on 8 November, he confided to a purring Andrew Marr that the army was deeply vexed by Corbyn's unilateralism, which damaged 'the credibility of deterrence'. On the same show, Maria Eagle, a PLP sniper with a seat on the front bench as the shadow defence secretary, told Marr that she agreed with the general. The *Sunday Times* had previously run an anonymous interview with 'a senior serving general'. 'Feelings are running very high within the armed forces,' the general was quoted as saying, about the very idea of a Corbyn government. 'You would see ... generals directly and publicly challenging Corbyn over ... Trident, pulling out of NATO and any plans to emasculate and shrink the size of the armed forces ... There would be mass resignations at all levels ... which would effectively be a mutiny. You can't put a maverick in charge of a country's security.'

There were no expressions of outrage at the attempted pre-emptive strike beyond a weak and weasely editorial in the *Guardian*. When Corbyn tried to complain to the Ministry of Defence, the response was that since his own colleague on the Labour front bench had agreed with the general, there was nothing they could do. A letter of complaint to Cameron elicited no sympathy whatsoever and a former Tory grandee, Ken Clarke, declared that the army was not answerable to parliament, but to the Queen.

In December 2015, Cameron sought parliamentary approval for sending British planes to bomb Islamic State in Syria. From his point of view, a happy possible side effect of the predictably successful vote was that it might make Corbyn's position as leader untenable. Having been shafted by Maria Eagle he was about to be stabbed in the front by Hilary Benn, whose disingenuous speech – Hitler, with the Spanish Civil War thrown in for good measure – was loudly cheered by Tory and hardcore Blairite MPs.

But this, too, failed to unseat Corbyn. The Labour leader – wrongly, in my opinion – permitted a free vote on the insistence of close colleagues. John McDonnell, the shadow chancellor, insisted it was a 'matter of conscience'. In the end sixty-six Labour MPs voted with the Tories to bomb targets in Syria. Some of them had been given presentations by the Ministry of Defence designed to convince them that there would be no collateral damage. But the majority of the PLP opposed the bombings and voted with Corbyn.

Frustrated yet again, the media sought to attribute the failure of more Labour MPs to vote for the bombing to the 'bullying' of the Stop the War Coalition (STW), an organization of which Corbyn had been the chair since the death of Tony Benn. For a week or so it was open season on the anti-war coalition. One effect was to scare the Green Party and cause the coalition's former leader, Caroline Lucas, to resign. Was this really her own decision or was it the idea of the inept Natalie Bennett, fearful that Green supporters were being carried away by the pied piper of Islington? Or was it a secret briefing from the deep state folk? Corbyn himself remained unmoved: he told the audience at a STW fundraising dinner that he was proud of the work the organization had done from the time of the Afghan war onwards, and that he was proud to serve as its chair.

Nevertheless, David Cameron and Corporal Benn got their way. British bombers at the Akrotiri base in Cyprus were dispatched to join the bombing queue. Since the skies above Syria were already jammed with NATO and Russian bomber jets, British intervention judged by its own criteria was unnecessary and its effects have certainly been limited. When they did bomb the northern Syrian city of Raqqa, local human rights monitors (hostile to both the jihadis and Assad), who were already being hunted down by Isis, declared that British bombs had killed dozens of civilians. The MoD disregarded their verdict and declared them a 'hostile source'. What might constitute a friendly source?

The Oldham by-election was scheduled for the same week as the Syria vote. This had, again, been talked up as a possible disaster for Corbyn. George Eaton in the *New Statesman* claimed to have been told by 'an insider' that 'defeat was far from unthinkable'. It was instead a resounding victory, leaving Corbyn's enemies on the defensive. How long could Labour MPs carry on this war on their own leader? Corbyn would not be bullied or demoralized.

The snipers will use any ammunition to achieve their goal. Bad local election results? The elections to the Scottish Parliament? Corbyn's fault? Of course. The zombies running Scottish Labour presided over the 2015 meltdown, the worst defeat since Labour was founded. But when they lost this time, it was Corbyn who was to blame.

What the Corbyn factor shows is that the centre of politics in England has moved far to the right since the 1980s. As a consequence the Corbyn–McDonnell economic programme, although in all honesty not very radical, nevertheless causes a break with the consensus established by Thatcher, Blair–Brown and Cameron. What it offers on the domestic front is a little bit of social democracy to strengthen the welfare state and a modest, fiscally manipulated form of income distribution. Despite this, the rupture shows that the thoughts and habits that have dominated the culture for almost four decades constitute a serious obstacle: private better than public, individual more important than society, rich more attractive than poor, a symbiosis of big money and small politics.

Many who concentrate their fire on Corbyn's supposed unelectability shy away from its corollary: under the present dispensation there is no room for any progressive alternative. The dogmatic vigour with which the EU and its Troika push back against any attempts by the left to shift the obstacle has contributed to a disturbing growth of the right in France, the Netherlands and now Germany, as well as to the election of hard-right governments in Hungary, Poland, Slovakia and Croatia. This is in part a result of the refusal to tolerate even a modicum of social democracy.

This is why the creation of a movement like Momentum is so interesting. This self-styled 'network of people and organizations to continue the energy and enthusiasm of Jeremy Corbyn's campaign' united old Bennites long asleep in the Labour Party with young activists drawn into action by the leadership contest. Since its formation in 2015 it has helped to build support by working within existing campaigns against war and austerity, registering voters, encouraging school-leavers and students to become politically active, and regularly debating opposing views (and not just on social networks). Only a movement of the sort that elected Corbyn as leader could send him to Downing Street.

During the Blair–Brown period the Labour Party unlearned social democracy of the Crosland variety, leave alone anything resembling the classical model of early socialism. Corbyn knows it's vital that the party relearns social democracy. It once seemed a hopeless task. Now, amazingly, they have a chance. The statistics about global inequality desperately need someone who can explain them in terms that can anger, mobilize and inspire people. If Corbyn can do this, it would mark an important shift in English politics.

However, Corbyn's radicalism lies not so much in what he is proposing on the domestic front – for that is increasingly the common sense of many economists and others, including the self-declared democratic socialist Bernie Sanders – but in his desire to change foreign policy.

The tens of thousands who flocked to join Corbyn's Labour Party were not that different from those who moved to support the SNP in the 2015 parliamentary elections, decimating Labour north of the border, after decades of taking such support for granted. The SNP's parliamentary cohort in Westminster provides solid support to the Labour left on a number of issues and will, no doubt, do so again when the Tories bring the projected renewal of Trident to the Commons.

In Scotland, there is a large majority in favour of the removal of nuclear missiles from Scottish shores. Elsewhere in the UK, public opinion is more evenly divided and fluctuates depending on the way the question is posed. A number of retired generals have questioned Trident's utility, and in his memoirs even Blair admitted that, in terms of both cost (£31 billion, with another £10 billion in reserve and lifetime costs predicted to exceed £180 billion) and utility, both 'common sense and practical argument' dictated getting rid of it. He was opposed to doing so because it would be 'too big a downgrading of our status as a nation'.

Further afield, his criticism of the absurdly high level of military expenditure is echoed by some prominent US economists in relation to their own country. Joseph Stiglitz and Linda Bilmes have argued that America's spending on wars since 2003, estimated now at nearly $8 trillion, is crippling the country. Yet such opinions when voiced by Corbyn and his circle are denounced as anti-American, extremist, a threat to Britain. Corbyn has long been hostile to both NATO and the EU as presently constituted, but his views on these matters are so alien to the PLP that they have for the time being been shelved.

Following the Brexit referendum, the PLP saw another chance to question Corbyn's authority. A year after his triumph his parliamentary colleagues turned on him again. They humiliated him, hoping that he would resign and save them the task of challenging him again. Arrogant, stupid, blinded by political hatred and behaving like a reactionary clerical estate, the PLP passed a no-confidence motion in him, ignoring the fact that the party membership had expressed no confidence in them by electing Corbyn in the first place. Corbyn did not budge.

This time the standard-bearer of reaction, the only person who stayed the course and challenged Corbyn for the party leadership, was Owen Smith, promoted by Ed

Miliband and forced to mouth absurdist rhetoric. So desperate was he that at one point he claimed to be 'more revolutionary than Corbyn'. He didn't believe this nonsense himself. Nor did anybody else. Corbyn won again.

The 2017 general election results saw a partial return to the two-party system in the United Kingdom. Labour had successfully presented a social democratic alternative to neoliberalism. Europhilia helped neither the Greens nor the Liberal Democrats nor the SNP. In the last case the Labour and Conservative vote registered a rise in Scotland, scuttling any possibility of another referendum on Scottish independence and breaking the SNP monopoly of representation that had been such a striking manifestation of their hegemony in 2015. Veering towards the extreme centre and draping herself in the EU flag did the party no favours.

The result was political earthquake. Andrew Murray, seconded from the UK's largest trade union, UNITE, to work as a senior adviser to the Corbyn campaign, explained Labour's success in an interview that I conducted with him in the weeks afterwards:

TARIQ ALI: You were at the heart of this campaign that won more and more support with every passing week and now many feel that another fortnight and Labour might have ended as the single largest party in parliament.

ANDREW MURRAY: It was a struggle. When the campaign began, Labour polling at 25 to 27 per cent – that was probably not wholly inaccurate at the time. We had local elections at the start of May 2017 where Labour didn't do particularly well, and many in the party were thinking we faced an impending electoral disaster. But, over the last month, we gained steadily in the polls – an atmosphere of increasing, I suppose, excitement in the campaign.

It's very frenetic. There are lots of small frictions and difficulties that pop up on a daily basis. But when you could see the huge reaction Jeremy Corbyn was getting as he went round the country, at events that were largely unreported on the broadcast, let alone the print, media, you had a sense of a mood really changing in the country. And, of course, the best polls by the end of it were putting us at 39/40 per cent, and even that slightly underestimated the final result. We began to wonder whether we might pull it off ... it felt like a real battle, with more and more wind in our sails. Our message was cutting through.

TA: And what of Corbyn himself?

AM: Well, he's extremely resilient, committed to his principles. A conviction politician. He's very comfortable in his own skin, very happy explaining and defending his views. All that came through in the campaign. The attacks on him, you would have to go back to the attacks on Tony Benn in the 1970s, Arthur Scargill in the 1980s, to see a similar level of vitriol. But it did not work this time. And one of the happy outcomes of this election is that progressive politicians in Britain need not be afraid of the *Sun* and the *Daily Mail*. They have thrown their worst at Jeremy Corbyn. They've abused him. They've described him on the one hand as a pacifist, the other hand a terrorist sympathizer, as if the two were somehow compatible. There's a new generation of young people who voted overwhelmingly for us – and this, on a record turnout for young people – for whom these smears simply do not work. It shows the sort of cynicism of the neoliberal political culture that has evolved.

There are two stars of the Labour campaign: one was Jeremy Corbyn and the second was the manifesto. And you'd have to go back I-don't-know-when to actually find a general election in Britain where the manifestos of any parties were of any consequence at all. They were only read by civil servants and policy wonks. And the conventional wisdom was manifestos don't matter, it's all to do with the presentation of the leader and how effectively you smear your opponents.

This was absolutely different. As soon as the manifesto came out you could see Labour's poll ratings starting to tick upwards. There was also the promise to build a million new homes, which is a huge issue, particularly in London, where housing is really priced-out for very many young people. Introduce a living wage of £10 an hour, and put a lot more money into the National Health

Service, which is creaking under a sort of semi-privatization, semi-starvation of funding policies. And all of these did really cut through.

An important consequence of this election is it marks the breakdown of the neoliberal consensus. In a way, I think 2017 saw politics catching up with 2008, the economic crash, which really meant that the neoliberals of the left and the right had nothing much left to offer. Often, there's a lag between an economic crisis – I'm referring to the Wall Street crash of 2008 – and politics. We can see it happening now. Young people could see there was an alternative, both here with Corbyn and Sanders in the United States – though the latter was successfully sabotaged by the Clinton–Obama wing of the Democrats.

TA: With the campaign well underway, we then saw two terrorist attacks, in Manchester and London. Virtually all the pundits thought that this would finish Corbyn off. Why should it? And that speech he made after Manchester was in some ways the most thoughtful and powerful speech of the campaign, explaining very cogently and carefully, without exaggeration, what is happening here: we hate it, it's despicable, it has to be dealt with but there are reasons and causes for it, which is our presence in the wars in those countries and what we have done to 'radicalize' the situation. Of course, there was another round of 'Corbyn blames Britain' for attacks, but they dropped that argument very quickly because the Tories must have done some private polling and realized their calumnies were not going down too well.

AM: Partly, it is about treating the British public like adults. Obviously campaigning had to be suspended for two or three days after that. And when we resumed, Jeremy took a view that it would be foolish to just pick up talking about pensions or the NHS or whatever you'd been doing. You had to address what had happened, and address it in a mature and measured way that makes no concession to excusing or trying to explain away the crime, but looks at why this is still happening, why sixteen years into a war on terror atrocities like this are still occurring. And I don't think he or anyone is arguing it could be traced back to one simple cause or there is now, if there ever was, one simple thing that could be done that would stop this. But, certainly, he was drawing attention to the fact we've had a war on terror that has failed – that actually it has not just failed it has made things worse in the sense of creating failed states throughout the region – and remembering that in 2001, al-Qaeda, or groups like it, really were entrenched only in Afghanistan.

And, so, he was drawing attention to that and saying we have to stop a foreign policy that is not making things better, but is in some respects making it a lot worse. And this was a mature argument. It would have been much easier just to say this is awful, we must simply condemn it and rely on anti-terrorist measures.

But, of course, when he made the speech the Conservatives responded in a knee-jerk way – 'You're blaming Britain', 'You're blaming us for this' – which of course was not what he was saying at all. There could be no reading of his speech that actually sustained that interpretation. And then there was a public poll on the day, which revealed that around 60 per cent of people thought he was right and 21 per cent thought he was wrong, and the rest had no opinion.

Corbyn's path to Downing Street is littered with thorns, but if the present is any indication, he will get there and sooner than we can imagine. The main problem for Corbyn is not the electorate or the members of the Labour Party. The obstructionists of Blairite and Brownite persuasion control the PLP and the party bureaucracy. Regional honchos have the power still to disband local parties. Of the electoral gains made in the last general elections there were only two MPs who could be described as left social democrats. Were Labour to win the next election the enemy would be within its ranks.

As Andrew Murray commented elsewhere:

> The PLP remains a bastion of reactionary politics. The 'soft left' still loathes Corbyn. The views and enthusiasms of the new members are yet to be reflected in parliament. The party bureaucracy that did its best to sabotage and defeat Corbyn from within is clinging on to its positions. The press has

already begun to start a campaign against 'far-left plots' to take over constituency parties. Soon there will be campaigns against the new economic policies being proposed by John McDonnell. Simultaneously, the Tories are trying to steal a few of Corbyn's clothes.

Meanwhile, across the Channel another election saw the virtual wipeout of the traditional conservative and socialist parties and the emergence of a banker as the new president, as well as the highest vote (just under 20 per cent) achieved by a left-wing candidate since 1969. European politics are refusing to settle down.

4

Euroland in Trouble

'A map of the world that does not include Utopia is not worth even glancing at,' Oscar Wilde once wrote, 'for it leaves out the one country at which humanity is always landing. And when humanity lands there, it looks out, and seeing a better country, sets sail. Progress is the realization of Utopias.'

Wilde's spirit is very much alive in the collective heart of the young who have come out onto the streets in protest against the forms of capitalism that have dominated the world since the Berlin Wall came down in 1989. They shouted their demands against the 1 per cent in New York, against US-backed dictatorship in Cairo, against the corruptions of the extreme centre in Greece and Spain, and for self-determination in Scotland.

The European Union – one of the largest economic enti-
ties on the planet, occupying a space greater than that of
the Roman Empire 2,000 years ago – is in a mess. All the
cover-ups, the attempts to suggest that all is well, that the
sticking plaster heavily applied around the EU's entire
body signals a return to normality, are deeply unconvincing. The stars on the EU flag are beginning to fade. The
second tier of countries brought into the European Union
were faded from the very beginning, while the main
countries are surviving; but for how long? The failure
of Europe's philosophers (Habermas and Negri come to
mind) to understand and analyse the nature of the crisis
indicates that they are part of the problem. Europe is not a
good abstraction. It is a bad reality, in which forces on the
extreme right have until recently dominated the debate.

How did the EU come about? What were its aims? It's
very difficult to provide single answers, because different
countries had different ideas about what happened and
why. The United States wanted the European countries
they had rescued during the Second World War, then
funded through the Marshall Plan, to be a bulwark of the
Cold War against the Russians and Eastern Europe. For
the French, it was an attempt to forge an alliance with
Germany. For the Germans, it was essential to German
exports. In addition, General de Gaulle, the French leader
who gave the final nod of approval to the Treaty of Rome,
regarded the Union contemptuously as nothing more
than a machine. He was not in favour of France's identity

and sovereignty being taken away in any shape or form. And nor has it been, until recently.

The father of the European Union was a very remarkable Frenchman, a cosmopolitan operator called Jean Monnet, whose record in economics, politics and social activities is quite entertaining. He was very close to the key cold warriors in the United States – Dean Acheson, the Dulles brothers, McCloy, among others. He was at once a French patriot and an internationalist. In *The New Old World*, a peerless account of modern Europe, Perry Anderson provides us with a diverting vignette of Monnet's early life. A stickler for propriety is one thing he never was:

> Monnet's marriage gives perhaps the best glimpse of his life, still only visible in part, between the wars. In 1929 he was floating a municipal bond in Milan, at the behest of John McCloy, when he fell in love with the newly wed wife of one of his Italian employees. There was no divorce under Mussolini, and a child was born to the married couple two years later. Attempts to get the marriage annulled were resisted by the husband and father, and refused by the Vatican. By 1934 Monnet's headquarters were in Shanghai. There one day he headed for the Trans-Siberian to meet his lover in Moscow, where she arrived from Switzerland, acquired Soviet citizenship overnight, dissolved her marriage, and wed him under the banns of the USSR. His bride, a devout Catholic, preferred these unusual arrangements – Monnet explained – to the demeaning offices

of Reno. Why Stalin's government allowed them, he could never understand. It was a tense time for a wedding: Kirov was assassinated a fortnight later. Subsequently, when her repudiated Italian spouse attempted to recover his four-year-old daughter in Shanghai, Madame Monnet found refuge from the kidnapper in the Soviet consulate – an establishment of some fame in the history of the Comintern. By the end of 1935, still holding a Soviet passport, she obtained residence in the US, when Monnet relocated to New York, on a Turkish quota. We are in the corridors of *Stamboul Train* or *Shanghai Express*.[1]

Monnet's adventures aside, the Western European unity was the offspring of the Second World War and the advent of the 'cold war' between the US and the Soviet Union that followed the defeat of the Axis powers. At its heart, in contrast to the horrors unleashed by the Treaty of Versailles that followed the First World War, was the notion of Franco-German unity, as equal partners; but in reality a key aim was to curb German political sovereignty. The existence of the Soviet Union and its newly acquired Eastern European satellites made any collective punishment of the wartime German elite impossible. The fact that the country had been divided was considered sufficient to prevent the rebirth of German militarism. Konrad Adenauer, the German conservative leader, was never convinced of the viability of East Germany

---

1   Perry Anderson, *The New Old World* (London and New York, 2009), p. 13.

and foresaw a reunification long before Gorbachev had become a twinkle in Reagan's eye.

De Gaulle was in favour of a tightly knit Europe, an independent Bonapartist bloc dealing with the USSR and the US in even-handed fashion and taking its own independent initiatives on the domestic and foreign policy fronts. For this reason he wanted to exclude Britain, since he (and almost everybody else) knew it would be little more than a Trojan horse for the United States. Both leaders were proved right. Today Germany is the strongest country in Europe, despite its truncated sovereignty, and the EU, expanded out of control as a result of Anglo-American pressure, is groaning like a sick bull.

Early attempts by the Frenchman Jacques Delors to create a 'social Europe' foundered on the born-again fanaticism of the Washington Consensus: neoliberal capitalism was the only way forward. The EU had to accept the new rules: privatizations at home, wars and occupations abroad. The Northern Europeans (Britain and Scandinavia) and the East Europeans (delighted to accept new satellite status, with the US replacing the USSR) proved to be the most loyal and compliant of the EU vassal states. The result has been a disaster for the EU as a whole.

Domestically it has become a Bankers' Europe, with little regard for anything but the needs of finance capital. The consequent economic crisis has not yet produced any real shift in the basic paradigm. A bandage drenched in antiseptic liquids has been applied to the wound, but the blood is still visible and will soon burst through again.

Seven years on from the crash of 2008, the American and European economies remain mired in unemployment and stagnation. The anarchy of credit creation has been brought under some control, but its foundations remain as solid as ever. Bankers, crooks, cheats are waiting patiently for the recovery so that they can resume their work with minimal regulation. And as if to reassure them, the Germans decided to reward Luxembourg – the money-laundering centre of the European rich – by elevating its star politician, Jean-Claude Juncker, to the post of president of the European Council.

The inability of Western rulers to drastically reform the system has led to an exacerbation of the crisis that now threatens the very functioning of democracy. In Greece and Italy, bankers govern the country. The social layer that created the crisis is now supplying bureaucrats to override politics. Elsewhere the extreme centre exercises power, promoting austerity measures that privilege the wealthy, and backing wars and occupations abroad. President Obama is far from isolated within the Euro-American political sphere, but new movements are now springing up at home, challenging political orthodoxies without offering a solution of their own.

How did we get here? Following the collapse of communism in 1991, money corrupted politics, and big money corrupted it absolutely. Throughout the heartlands of capital we witnessed the emergence of effective coalitions: as ever, the Republicans and Democrats in the United States; New Labour and Tories in Britain; Socialists and a medley of conservatives in France; the German coalitions of one variety or another, with the Greens differentiating themselves largely as ultra-Atlanticists; the virtually identical Scandinavian centre-right and centre-left, competing in cravenness before the Empire. In almost every case the two/three-party system morphed into an effective national government.

A new market extremism came into play. The entry of capital into the most hallowed domains of social provision was touted as a necessary 'reform'. Private finance initiatives that punished the public sector became the norm, and countries (such as France and Germany) that were seen as not proceeding fast enough in the direction of the neoliberal paradise were regularly denounced in the *Economist* and the *Financial Times*. To question this turn, to defend the public sector, to argue in favour of state ownership of utilities, to challenge the fire sale of public housing, was to be regarded as a 'conservative' dinosaur.

The politicians of the extreme centre, intoxicated by the triumphs of capitalism, were unprepared for the 2008 crisis. So were most citizens, hoodwinked by the availability of easy loans and a tame, uncritical media into believing that all was well. Their leaders might not be charismatic, but they knew how to handle the system. Leave it all to the politicians. The price for this institutionalized apathy is now being paid. (To be fair, the Irish, Dutch and French peoples scented disaster in the arguments over the EU constitution that enshrined neoliberalism, and voted against it. They were ignored.)

Yet it was obvious to many economists that Wall Street deliberately pumped up the housing bubble, spending billions on advertising campaigns to encourage people to take out second mortgages and increase personal debt, in order to spend blindly on consumer goods. The bubble had to burst, and when it did the system tottered until the state rescued the banks from total collapse. When the crisis spread to Europe, all single-market and competition rules were flushed down the toilet as the EU mounted its salvage operation. The disciplines of the market were now conveniently forgotten.

As some countries collapsed (Iceland, Ireland, Greece) and others (Portugal, Spain, Italy) stared into the abyss, the EU stepped in to impose austerity and to save the German, French and British banking systems. The tensions between the market and democratic accountability could no longer be masked.

The Greek elite was blackmailed into total submission, while the austerity measures thrust down the throats of the citizenry brought the country to the brink of revolution. Greece is the weakest link in the chain of European capitalism, its democracy long submerged beneath the waves of capitalism in crisis. General strikes and creative protests have made the task of the extreme centre very difficult.

Today, the fog of confusion has finally lifted and people are searching for alternatives, but without involving political parties, since virtually all of these have been found wanting. The occupations staged in many countries were very different from the protests of the past. These were actions mounted in times of growing unemployment and in places where the future looks grim. A majority of young people will not get a higher education unless they can conjure up considerable sums; soon, no doubt, they will be confronted with a two-tier health system. Capitalist democracy today presupposes a fundamental agreement between the main parties represented in parliament, so that their bickering, limited by their moderation, becomes utterly insignificant. The ideology can be called democratism, but democracy itself offers no real alternatives.

The occupations and street protests against capitalism are in some ways analogous to the peasant jacqueries of preceding centuries. Unacceptable conditions lead to uprisings, which then are usually crushed or subside of their own accord. What is important is that they are often harbingers of what is to come if conditions do not improve. No movement can survive unless it creates a permanent democratic structure to maintain political continuity. The greater the popular support for any such movement, the greater the need for some form of organization.

The South American rebellions against neoliberalism and its global institutions are telling models in this regard. Huge and successful struggles against the IMF in Venezuela, against water privatization in Bolivia, and against electricity privatization in Peru, created the basis for a new politics that triumphed at the polls in the first two countries, as well as in Ecuador and Paraguay. Once elected, the new governments began to implement the promised social and economic reforms with varying degrees of success.

The advice proffered to the Labour Party in Britain in 1958 by Professor H. D. Dickinson was rejected by Labour, but accepted by the Bolivarian leaders in Venezuela and Bolivia some forty years later:

> If the welfare state is to survive, the state must find a source of income of its own, a source to which it has a claim prior to that of ... a profits-receiver. The only source that I can see is that of productive property. The state must come, in some way or another, to own a very large chunk of the land and capital of the country. This may not be a popular policy: but, unless it is pursued, the policy of improved social services, which is a popular one, will become impossible. You cannot for long socialize the means of consumption unless you first socialize the means of production.

The rulers of the world will see in these words little more than an expression of utopianism, but they would be wrong. For these are the structural reforms that are really needed, not those being pushed by the EU. What is needed is a complete turnaround, preceded by a public admission that the Wall Street system could not and did not work and has to be abandoned.

Gaullist France had wanted the European Union to become a neutral force, and some in Germany felt the same. If Europe developed as a major power, then it could act as a balance between the Russians and the Americans in the Cold War. It could strike out on its own, with an independent politics and independent positions and an independent way of organizing society. This was a much-supported idea in the European Union, one that developed slowly.

But soon the inevitable happened: the reunification of Germany, predicted by German chancellor Adenauer to de Gaulle as early as the 1950s, changed the face of Europe once again. A unified Germany became the dominant European power and despite the faux modesty, the German elite enjoyed stepping back into the limelight. The United States perceived that the only way now to prevent Europe from becoming too powerful was to dilute and expand the union, making any serious economic and political federation impossible.

They had always known that, sooner or later, reviving these economies would produce countries that would rival the US, at least on the economic and trade fronts. They had been prepared to take that risk because, while the Soviet Union persisted, it seemed as if there was no other effective way to shore up the frayed postwar capitalist system. But when the Soviet Union self-destructed and was dismantled, new problems arose, partially political, but mostly social and economic. With the victory of Hayek and the Chicago School came the birth of what became known as neoliberalism.

Accordingly, the European Union began to determine the social and economic policies of its member states. This meant ending state control of industries, and slowly but inexorably dismantling the social welfare state by bringing the market into what had until now been the most hallowed domains of social provision.

Thus when the 2008 crisis exploded, the result was pure panic in EU headquarters. Panic in Berlin. Panic in Paris. Panic in London. What were they going to do? American economists argued that now was the time to reintroduce a form of Keynesianism, to stimulate the economy, and they did that to some degree in the United States. Not so in Europe, however, because here they had spent too much; too much was at stake – socially, economically, ideologically – for them to make that turn. So what we got instead were the austerity measures decided on by Berlin and backed by all the existing governments of the European Union: the poorer the country, the more craven its leaders.

The European Union is now confronting a social, political and economic crisis of some magnitude. Its only solution is to punish the victims. The extreme centre in most of the member states is there to make sure that this happens, and that oppositions are crushed – except when they emerge on the right.

Until the bubble bursts again it can be ignored, unless there is a huge revolt from below. As far as the rulers of Europe are concerned, everything is over, problem more or less solved. Those who predicted the collapse of the euro have been proved wrong. As long as the German banks are happy, the elites are happy. They think that they have managed to control the system. But the view is not so rosy when glimpsed from the beleaguered parliaments of Athens and Madrid; from the shuttered shops, barricaded buildings and boarded-up homes of Lisbon and Dublin. Even in the thriving metropolises – London, Paris, Brussels, Milan, Frankfurt – there are dark corners hidden from the public gaze. In these poorer quarters, inhabited by migrants, by the unemployed, by the homeless, life goes on and there is even a sense of community, missing elsewhere in the big city; but the problems of everyday subsistence permit little time for relaxation.

For the Troika-ruled EU countries, the single currency has turned into a shackle, tying more than half of the eurozone into permanent recession. Greece has been reduced to penury, its economy shrivelled by a fifth, wages down 50 per cent, massive youth unemployment. Two-thirds of young people are out of work. The Spanish experience is no better. A grandparent's pension or a single salary is used in many cases to sustain three generations.

Unemployment is running at 26 per cent, wages are not paid, the rate for casual labour in Spain is down to two euros an hour.

Italy has been in recession for a number of years, after a decade of economic stagnation. Today, 42 per cent of young Italians are without a job. In Portugal, tens of thousands of small family businesses, the backbone of the Portuguese economy for many decades, have been forced to shut down. More than half of those out of work are not entitled to unemployment benefits. And in Ireland, yet again, the young, the best and brightest of this nation, have left. A sad repetition of the migrations that helped lock Ireland into conservatism and underdevelopment for decades.

The European Union is the instrument of the Council of Ministers. These ministers are governmental representatives, elected by their countries, in their parliaments, who determine everything. The democratic deficit in the European Union is therefore huge. The European Parliament has no effective power at all – bar the power to elect the president of the European Union, who, in turn, has no power at all. Power is still exercised by individual states, but if they should fall out it's not really a problem. Germany, as the richest and largest state of the EU, now plays the major role in determining economic policies. If the German bankers want austerity, the politicians in league with them ensure that their demands will be met, because this is effectively a bankers' union. The elites have made of the EU a system that serves their interests. It is an economic union that imposes economic policies, rather than a social or a political union.

In short, the European Union that has emerged from the epic battle to protect the euro is significantly more autocratic, more authoritarian, German-dominated and right-wing, while lacking any compensatory charm. And the eurozone continues to expand. Croatia joined the EU in 2011. That same year Estonia adopted the euro, as did Latvia in 2014. However, the new order has produced an ad hoc economic directorate with no legitimation beyond the emergency itself.

This directorate is what has been dubbed the Troika. It has no official name, but was assembled in April 2010 to take over direction of the Greek economy as the condition for the first loan. It's composed essentially of bureaucrats from the European Commission, the European Central Bank, and the International Monetary Fund. The Troika now governs Portugal, Ireland, Cyprus and Greece. And it has been permanently inscribed in the European stability mechanism. The Troika issues memoranda of understanding on the same model as the IMF, which dictates every detail of the member states' legislative programmes.

Each national government will ensure that the leg-islation for cuts in health, cuts in education, cuts in the public sector, redundancies, reductions in the state pension, removal of benefits from unemployed workers, is presented to and approved by parliament. The government will then present a privatization plan to parliament and ensure it is passed. And the Troika insists, in their own words, that the government will consult ex-ante on the adoption of policies not included in this memorandum. The only way to describe this is financial semi-colonialism.

The Troika's record for economic management has been abysmal. Greek gross domestic product was forecast to fall by 5 per cent from 2009 to 2012; it dropped by 17 per cent and is still going down. Unemployment was supposed to peak at 15 per cent in 2012, it passed 25 per cent. A V-shaped recovery was forecast for 2012, with Greek debt falling to sustainable levels; instead, the debt burden is larger than ever. No one challenges the Troika except the people on the streets, represented by parties like Syriza in Greece. This party, the only real alternative that has emerged since the crisis, is now on the verge of coming to power. It did extremely well in the European elections. The emergence of Podemos in Spain as the movement most likely to win the popular vote is another straw in the wind (discussed more fully in the afterword).

Elsewhere, it's the parties of the extreme right that have benefited. They have developed two interrelated arguments. First, that it is EU policies which have led to austerity and hurt the poor, and second, that the free movement of labour from EU countries with low wages and high unemployment makes conditions much worse.

With regard to the second point, immigration is a set of policies that have been accepted for centuries. The world would not be what it is today were it not for immigration. German companies wanted Turkish labour, France imported people from its former colonies to work in French industries, the British government sent Enoch Powell to the West Indies to recruit nurses for the new National Health Service. All this has been happening for ages, so the notion that the people who are to blame for the crisis are the immigrants is a cheap, squalid, sordid prejudice that has no basis in reality. But today the right and the extreme right are saying that migrants coming from Poland and Romania – from the second tier of fading-star states – are actually taking our jobs away.

For that is one thing you sign up to when you sign up to the European Union. It's not only free movement of capital, it's free movement of labour within EU borders. And to get rid of that would severely damage many European economies. The politicians are aware of the fact, but it's always good to find scapegoats when the real reasons cannot be explained.

The irony confronting the leaders of the European Union is that they have created an economic system in large parts of Europe which is not functioning properly, and that people are turning away in droves from the political superstructure whose main aim is to defend the system at all costs. Young people, in particular, are not interested in mainstream politics. Large numbers don't vote any more. And this is the fault, not of the union as such, but of the bankers that control it and determine the policies which member states have to follow.

The EU is the mother ship of the extreme centre, with this difference: unlike its subsidiary vassals, it is not responsible to any elected body. This crisis is not going to go away. The further cuts scheduled for the Troika-controlled countries in 2015 lack the slightest economic rationale. A set of unelected bureaucrats, working for banks, the IMF, the ECB, etc., are telling independent governments: this is what you can do and this is what you can't do. They are in some cases removing prime ministers and putting new prime ministers in their place.

If this is the situation, then things cannot possibly get better. If unelected bankers are deciding upon the needs of people in a number of European countries, as they are, how can things move forward? But this is not something understood today by the uncritical defenders of Europe. For them, there's nothing wrong, Europe is great, it's a great idea, don't do anything to it.

A recent example is the liberal manifesto *For Europe!* composed by the German Green Daniel Cohn-Bendit and a former Belgian prime minister, Guy Verhofstadt. The two men write:

Only the European Union is able to guarantee the social rights of all European citizens and to eradicate poverty. Only Europe can solve the problems of globalization, climate change and social injustice. The shining example of Europe has inspired other continents to go down the path of regional cooperation. No continent is better equipped to renounce its violent past and strive for a more peaceful world.

Which Europe could they be looking at? This is a view from inside the bubble. Even in Germany, the strongest of the EU states, there is growing unease with the role the nation is being forced to play and a number of anti-EU parties have emerged. Most of these parties are misguided, but the reason they have arisen is the pervasive loss of trust in the elites who control party politics and represent the symbiosis between big banks, big corporations and politics, all umbilically linked. Hostility to the EU is not confined to the far right. It is the failure of both the extreme centre and many on the left to sharply criticize the EU that has made the right such a pole of attraction.

Far from being the case that criticizing a hallowed EU will encourage reaction and national chauvinism, it is the lack of a serious critique that is exacerbating the process. Habermas is, of course, a philosopher of the extreme centre. Negri should know better. The gulf between Europe's rulers and the ruled has rarely been starker. Politically, the absence of any democratic accountability in the structures of the EU combines badly with the economics of debt-logged stagnation. On the military front, membership of NATO is virtually compulsory for new members, slotting them in to a broader imperial strategy. German unification, celebrated all over the EU, has led to the country becoming the key state in determining social and economic priorities.

Member-state equality became a joke after the expansion. Even when in two founding states, France and Holland, majorities voted against the EU constitution in 2005 mainly because it enshrined neoliberalism, popular opinion as expressed in those referenda was effectively ignored. Currently the Berlin–Washington Axis overrides the archaic and authoritarian structures of the European Union in the eventuality of major policy disagreements. The Franco-German equilibrium has become meaningless and redundant. Once German decisions get the green light from Washington, they are imposed on the other member states.

Most of Europe's admired philosophers cannot interpret this world, let alone change it. Economists and sociologists, however, are discussing a number of possible alternatives. In 'EuroMemorandum 2014', a group of radical European economists have mapped an alternative course of action.[2] Their criticisms focus on the failed economic policies, pointing out that youth unemployment in 2013, while relatively low in Germany (7.8 per cent) and

2   Online at www.euromemorandum.eu.

Austria (9.1 per cent) was 23.7 per cent in Belgium, 25.8 per cent in France and Ireland, 57.3 per cent in Greece and 55.9 per cent in Spain. In the sphere of finance, the economists note that the situation is 'extremely fragile' and that in Italy and Spain, the new 'government bond issues have been taken up almost entirely by nationally-based banks'. On banking reform they insist that the 'weight of finance in the economy' must be reduced and speculation made illegal in the banking system.

Most of their arguments, especially those sharply critical of the authoritarian imposition of 'structural reforms' under threat of sanctions, are cogent and rational. They call for an end to sado-monetarism. But who will bring about the changes they recommend? Not the politicians of the extreme centre, not the ECB and its satellites, and not the US Treasury or the Federal Reserve. It may be hoped that the growth of social movements and the likely success of radical European parties, like Syriza and Podemos, at the polls may lead to a serious discussion of an alternative economics – but any such development will be hindered by each and every structure of the European Union. It does not permit an opposition. Fear and intimidation will be much in evidence if these parties win.

The multitudes were largely passive when the Treaty of Rome was signed. They're rather more feisty now, of course, but usually on the side of the right, as in France, Holland, Germany and Italy. Only in Spain and Greece, both countries with a long experience of civil war and dictatorship, have we seen the possibility of something different. A challenge to the extreme centre from the left, but an untried left that has yet to be tested. It would be an error if they simply accepted the legitimacy of the EU and its institutions as presently constituted. The German sociologist Wolfgang Streeck has, in the final chapter of his *Buying Time*, sketched the outline of what form a new, democratic European Constitution could take, representing as the continent does a culturally diverse and socially heterogeneous reality. The merchants of the status quo have granted the European Parliament some more powers, but not sovereignty. The largest caucus in the Parliament used this to elect the Luxembourger, Jean-Claude Junker, as the new president. A politician who authorized the tiny duchy to launder money and made it a tax haven for the rich was a symbolic choice. It was to be business as usual.

Who is going to snip the umbilical cord? The extreme right or new forces on the left? This remains the great unanswered question. The future of many EU countries, and indeed of the European Union itself (as constituted at present), will depend on the course taken by the crisis in the years ahead.

5

Natopolis

On 5 September 2014, in Newport, Wales, the North Atlantic Treaty Organization held an emergency conclave. The aim of the summit was to discuss how to deal with ISIS, the Islamic State of Iraq and Syria; but beneath this primary concern there were other considerations. Should NATO prepare a rapid deployment force enabling it to send in a few thousand soldiers, commandos backed by air power, wherever it was necessary to defend Western interests and the Global Empire? Or should it scale down its operations and accept that its interventions in Afghanistan and elsewhere had been a failure?

Nobody was much concerned about this failure, but rather focused their attention on how to keep the organization going and give it a raison d'être, one that would make sense to a sceptical public opinion. From that point of view, the conclave could not have found a better enemy than ISIS. Here was an organization creating telegenic havoc, pandering to every conceivable stereotype of the Islamic terrorist. Such an enemy could prove useful for pushing through a number of important policy changes. And so it came to pass.

It is therefore worth considering what NATO is, what it was and what it might become. NATO was set up in 1949, soon after the end of the Second World War. Its aim was a simple one, bluntly expressed in the words of Winston Churchill's leading military adviser, Lord Ismay: 'NATO was designed to keep *the Americans in*, *the Russians out*, and *the Germans down*.' Has anything much changed since then?

According to its own rhetoric, NATO was primarily (in contrast to Lord Ismay's observation) designed to ward off any Soviet aggression against the Western democracies. But did anyone believe there was a real threat?

In practice NATO became a mechanism, controlled by the United States, whereby its European allies were kept under a military umbrella. And yet it is worth noting that throughout the Cold War years, from 1949 to 1990, NATO never fought a single battle. It was neither tried nor tested. Instead, it was a military propaganda organization, designed to control allies rather than punish enemies. Yet things changed following the fall of the

Berlin Wall. Where once the purpose was a defensive show of strength, it now became an offensive test of strength, giving rise to operational shifts and corresponding changes in its command structure. This was on public record at the Welsh summit in 2014.

There have been two and a half phases in NATO's development since 1949. The original members comprised the United States, the United Kingdom, Belgium, Canada, France, Denmark, Norway and Iceland. Iceland's inclusion is something of a mystery, because there was never any serious threat to Iceland – a country that doesn't even have a standing army. It was brought in effectively to accommodate strategic monitoring centres and military bases.

Then, in 1952, additions were made to the core countries: Turkey and Greece joined together, because they couldn't have Turkey without having Greece. The decisive year for NATO was 1955, when Washington decided to bring Germany into the Treaty. This invitation created a great debate within European society. All the French political parties were nervous that Germany was going to be rearmed, although the process had already started in previous years. The Russians were livid. Having lost twenty million people in the Second World War, they did not want to see a remilitarized Germany. Britain was on message, though left-wing Labour MPs led by Konni Zilliacus and Fenner Brockway protested strongly in the House of Commons. Even within West

Germany there was unease, but the decision was pushed through.

The reaction was predictable, and the Soviet Union set up their own version of NATO. Just as Western satellite states were in NATO, the East European satellite states were gathered into the Warsaw Pact. Nonetheless, Yugoslavia under Tito refused to join either organization, opening up a new space for non-aligned world politics. As a result, Cold War tensions were further racked up between the two power blocs.

What would NATO do next? The Spanish dictator General Franco had obstinately kept Spain out of NATO, unlike neighbouring Portugal. But in the post-Franco interregnum the Socialist Party leader, Felipe González, promised a referendum. At that time a large majority of the country was hostile to Spanish membership, and many of the campaigners against NATO were leading socialist politicians, including Javier Solana. But by the time the referendum took place in 1986 the socialist and conservative parties had united on the matter, both advocating NATO membership as a necessary step forward for Spain. The event also marked the birth of the extreme centre in the country: after a bitter campaign, 53 per cent voted for membership, 40.3 per cent against. In some areas such as Barcelona, however, the largest Mediterranean city and the capital of Catalonia, 51 per cent voted against. Javier Solana, formerly in opposition, then integrated into the Socialist Party leadership, was eventually crowned as NATO secretary general.

In France, General de Gaulle was never really happy about NATO. He saw it as dominated by the United States, backed by Britain, which was of course an undeniable fact. In 1966 de Gaulle pulled out of NATO, on the grounds that French independence was seriously compromised by membership. France has never been as respected as it was during that period. The situation changed in 2009, when President Sarkozy joined the integrated military command structure of NATO. Collaborations and cooperative undertakings with NATO had begun a long time before, but Sarkozy's decision effectively acknowledged that the French were now dominated by the United States. Former president François Hollande, who attended the last NATO summit, continues in this vein. Thus NATO has become a successful organization containing all the major European powers.

After the Cold War and the collapse of the Soviet Union – despite the promises to the contrary made to Gorbachev and Yeltsin – NATO moved eastwards, integrating Eastern European countries into the command structure of NATO and effectively making them dependent states. Those Eastern European states happily moved into their new position as US satellites, sanctified by their NATO membership. The large gathering in Wales included many Eastern European leaders.

But there was one problem: what was NATO's function

after the Cold War? Initially there was a great deal of talk about the 'peace dividend'. NATO could have been disbanded once and for all, like the Warsaw Pact; but this did not happen. A number of neoconservative ideologues, backed by Clinton, decided that NATO was necessary to keep the European powers under American influence. But they weren't tempted to act on their own, because the most important event at the end of the Cold War was the reunification of Germany, creating the largest, most powerful, most economically successful state of the European Union.

Meanwhile, in both France and Britain, conservative politicians began grumbling, talking about the Fourth Reich, and about how Germany could be stopped. The German leaders themselves insisted that they weren't planning anything, they only wanted to be part of the European Union. They clearly did not want any independence outside this collective of firm allies embedded inside the North Atlantic Treaty Organization.

However, faced with the growth of ethnic tensions and violence in Yugoslavia, the Germans acted unilaterally without consulting their colleagues. Against the advice of both Washington and London, they decided to break up Yugoslavia by interfering first with the Slovenes and subsequently with the Croats, recognizing Slovenia, recognizing Croatia, and effectively destroying the Yugoslav state.

The forthright German decision to exercise its influence in Central Europe worried the others. The United

States became interested militarily in the former Yugoslavia at this stage – as the country disintegrated. Clans started fighting each other, with atrocities taking place in Srebrenica when Bosnians were massacred by Serbian troops. At the same time, the ancient Serb community were expelled from Krajina in Croatia, something not talked about too much at the time. Finally NATO entered into the conflict by bombing Serbia.

The pretext for this aggression was that there were massacres taking place in Kosovo and these had to be stopped at all costs. At that time there were, in fact, very few massacres taking place there. The worst of the slaughter had already been perpetrated in Bosnia, and the West, no doubt regretting that it hadn't intervened at that time, now decided something had to be done in Kosovo.

The action taken by the Kosovan Liberation Army to provoke Serbian counterattacks was not totally successful, but this didn't prevent the propaganda apparatus of the West from comparing what was happening in Kosovo to 1940s Germany. They decided on a bombing campaign designed to break the back of the Serbian leadership. This bombardment actually led to a considerable number of casualties, but at that moment – most interestingly – NATO's bacon, if one can put it like that, was saved by Moscow.

Here, the Russians were decisive in preventing what could have been a major catastrophe for NATO. Moscow's refusal, under US pressure, to provide the Serbs with sophisticated anti-aircraft weapons to defend their country enabled the indiscriminate terror from the sky to continue unabated for several weeks. This was made clear by none other than Michael Ignatieff, a NATO hawk who wrote at the time in the *New Yorker*:

> Devastating as the execution of the air campaign proved to be, particularly against Serbia's civilian infrastructure, it might have turned out very differently if the Russians had given the Serbs their latest technology. The air war was essentially a duel between 70s Soviet air defence technology and state-of-the-art American precision guidance systems. If NATO had been up against 80s Soviet technology, it might have lost twenty planes, and it is unclear whether NATO's electorates would have stood for such losses.[1]

What made this surreal was the way it was fought exclusively from the skies. NATO dominated the airspace over the Balkans, but on a strictly military level it achieved very little. For the first weeks, every NATO politician spoke in semi-religious tones of degrading the Yugoslav army. This was stated to be a major war aim – but it was a dismal failure. Despite undergoing seventy-eight days of continuous bombardment and more than 36,000 sorties, the Yugoslav army emerged from Kosovo virtually

---

1 Michael Ignatieff, 'The Virtual Commander', *New Yorker*, 2 August 1999.

unscathed. The morale of the Serbian soldiers leaving Kosovo after the ceasefire appeared to be very high.

The first balance sheet of the war indicates that it went wrong at every level. There was no military victory. The Albright-led war party in Washington, which had decided to wage NATO's first war against a sovereign state in breach of all international regulations, was convinced that it would be at best a three-day affair; a short, sharp shock that would bring the leader of Serbia, Slobodan Milošević, to his knees. This did not happen. Serious divisions existed at the highest level of NATO, as a result of which even the question of targets could not be agreed on. The supreme commander, General Wesley Clark, was constantly at odds with the US air force and NATO chief, General Michael Short. Clark wanted to hunt down Serbian army units in Kosovo. Short favoured an easier option: to destroy the infrastructure within Serbia. When NATO planes bombed Belgrade, the following conversation took place between Clark and Short:

SHORT: This is the jewel in the crown.

CLARK: To me the jewel in the crown is when those B-52s rumble between Kosovo and Belgrade.

SHORT: You and I have known for weeks that we have different jewellers.

CLARK: My jeweller outranks yours.[2]

---

2   Dana Priest, 'United NATO Front Was Divided Within', *Washington Post*, 21 September 1999.

On the political level, all that NATO achieved had already been on offer from the Serbian leadership well before the beginning of the war. The provocative clauses of the Rambouillet Agreement, an open violation of Serb sovereignty, were inserted at the last minute to prevent a Serbian signature and thus enable NATO to show its muscle; they were not included in the ceasefire treaty.

The war in former Yugoslavia was essentially a war of NATO dominance, using a troubled Balkan state as a pretext. Its aim was to define NATO as a military enforcer in the new world order that was being created. It was not motivated by concern for the Kosovans or the Yugoslavs or the former Yugoslavia as a whole, but rather by the desire to assert US hegemony over its own allies. It was a shot across the bows of the German chancellery. No matter that the mess simply got worse; today, many of these countries are in a desperate state. It's a sorry picture all across Balkan lands, but no one talks about it.

This was NATO's first war; and did the high command learn anything? The United States, which effectively ran the military side of the operation, made it clear that such a war would never take place again where there were too many fingers on the trigger. They criticized French and other politicians for marching into command rooms and making what they saw as irrational demands.

Subsequently NATO has carried out other operations, such as in Afghanistan, which was another spectacular failure. If the goal was merely to get rid of the Taliban government, they could have walked out a year later. But the declared goal was to make Afghanistan into a modern state. In the months following the withdrawal from Afghanistan, the situation in that country grew dire. The army the occupiers created is totally unreliable. So by whatever criteria you judge it, NATO's war in Afghanistan and its occupation of that country, which has lasted over ten years, has been an unmitigated disaster.

In between, NATO found time to carry out a six-month bombing raid on Libya. The air attack destroyed the government, destroyed the infrastructure, overlooked the brutal lynching of Gaddafi – and then what? Hardly a week goes by without a news item about chaos in Libya, from jihadi groups controlling the airports, to the NATO-appointed prime minister being removed. In September 2014, the entire parliament created by the NATO people and their allies had to be evacuated from the parliament building in Tripoli and bundled to safety on a ship. What more striking image of 'democracy' than a NATO-created parliament floating on the Mediterranean, waiting for a country to rule?

Another Arab state wrecked, millions homeless, spreading turmoil in Africa, while the chaos in Iraq and Syria continues. And still the lessons aren't learned. So NATO's decision in Newport to deploy a rapid deployment force at short notice will change very little. The same people who were sent undercover to fight in Libya will now go openly, wherever needed. Much better to strip away the mask and let the citizens observe what is being done in their name. Perhaps one day they will stop sleepwalking and wake up. Meanwhile British commando units, American irregulars, 'advisers', and Blackwater mercenaries will be on call to carry out regime transplants.

Given this new transparency, it might be more honest for the United States to take total, overt command of NATO: it couldn't function without them, and they might as well reveal the EU without the fig leaf. George W. Bush was more relaxed on this question. He said, 'Well, look, we act as we see fit, when we see fit, through whatever organization we can. We try the United Nations Security Council, if it approves we go under the flag of the United Nations. If it doesn't, we use NATO. If there are differences within NATO, as there were in Iraq, we go it alone.'

Is there a possibility that NATO might crumble over the next few years? There's no sign of it so far. It would require Germany and France moving out, and there is no sign of this whatsoever. They want the fictions of NATO to remain in force; and sometimes the Pentagon rewards loyalty. The summits – like their G20, G8, EU, UN equivalents – are essentially a public relations exercise. They are not really needed, except to keep public opinion on side. The reality is that NATO, with or without a rapid deployment force, with or without the complete and unstinting support of its European allies on every mission or not, is effectively an instrument of the US, designed to preserve US hegemony and the global empire.

This does not mean that the United States controls each and every country in the most minute detail, like the European empires of preceding centuries, or their successor the Troika in relation to the economies of Greece and Portugal and Ireland today; that is not what the global empire is about. The global empire is the continued maintenance of US hegemony in a world where new forces are not rising up against it, but are certainly challenging it. Russia has defied it in the Ukraine; China is opposed to many US policies in the Pacific. Since NATO acts solely as the European arm of the global empire, other arms are being created in various shapes and forms in the Pacific zone, involving US bases in Japan and South Korea that are part and parcel of the same exercise. But trouble lies ahead. It is high time that the total failure in the Middle East, and the instability that reigns in that region despite – or because of – NATO interventions, begins to set off some serious debates within the US administration itself.

6

The Starship *Enterprise*

Britain became a semi-vassal state to the United States in 1945, as it began to dismantle its own empire. This subordination became clear in 1956, when it was told in no uncertain terms that military adventures without US support were not permitted: it was forced to withdraw from Egypt, which it had jointly invaded with Israel and France. Britain was granted full vassal status in 1980. The Malvinas/Falklands War would have been impossible without the support of Washington and one of its favoured South American satellites, General Pinochet's Chile.

Since British economic and foreign policies are now in tandem with those of its imperial master, British leaders sometimes attempt to stand out by pre-empting US decisions and posturing as being tougher on assorted 'enemies' than Washington itself.[1] As Edward Snowden has revealed, British intelligence-gathering outposts like GCHQ operate with impunity. The relative autonomy they enjoy – with less restraints than the NSA – is extremely useful for the latter, which treats GCHQ as a valued surrogate.

Similarly, till 2008, British politicians liked to boast that the local 'light-touch regulation' put the City of London well ahead of Wall Street, as Britain's current standing as a virtual tax haven still does, approaching Luxembourg levels if not yet those of the Cayman Islands. Given this reality, the right-wing obsession with the European Union seems a bit misplaced. It's with Washington (not Brussels) that London has long been stuck in the dog-like coital lock sometimes described as a 'special relationship'.

Given this reality, it's necessary to evaluate the strength and weakness of the American Empire, for the future of what was once the 'world-island' and its ruling class is dependent on US global hegemony.

For over three decades now the United States has been without a serious global rival. Temporary enemies – bit players attached to no state – have emerged, but failed to make a challenge. Meanwhile, flawed diagnoses of the state of the Empire proliferate like magic mushrooms: some glimpse imperial disintegration in the inner dislocations

---

1   Witness Thatcher in Eastern Europe, Blair in the Balkans and Middle East and, most recently, Cameron lecturing Putin on the Ukraine.

of American society; others argue from faith coupled with misinterpreted facts; still others overdose on ahistorical determinism, coated with political presuppositions that amount to little more than wishful thinking. Since all empires in human history have fallen, the American version will inevitably do so too. But when? Until now, despite many a setback, the signs of impending collapse or irreversible decline are few.

Occasionally, left-liberals and fellow travellers attempt to paint a canvas highlighting the setbacks in lurid colours, while leaving all else in darkness. The implication is that the United States was once an all-powerful empire but is now on the wane. The first claim of omnipotence was never the case, and a cold-eyed survey of the evidence suggests that the second assumption, too, is misjudged.

One conscious or sub-conscious function underlying this false optimism about the US's imminent decline is to abandon effective opposition. It's no longer necessary to ask questions. If an empire is approaching its death agony, why waste time discussing the real symptoms? Such an attitude encourages one to decontextualize geopolitical problems, seeing them in isolation from the strategy or needs of the grand hegemon. In this view the world becomes a chessboard, with the pawns in control. None of the setbacks suffered by the United States – most seriously in South America where the Bolivarians have a universal appeal, unlike the jihadis and their supporters – justifies such a view.

The fact is that the globe still revolves, however shakily, around a fixed political, ideological and military axis. We are not even close to the twilight years of the American imperium. Nor is Washington in any mood to surrender its place in the world. It may be a 'stationary state'[2] at home for the time being, but it is hyperactive abroad. In fact domestic economic problems, whose seriousness should not be underestimated, make the Empire more violent abroad. Each new enemy, however peripheral, is described as evil incarnate and presented as such by global media networks, like a capitalist variant of an old Stalinist category – the 'enemies of the people' who should be imprisoned, tortured or exterminated at will.

Epigones of various sorts justify each act as necessary to preserve Western civilization, by which they mean Capitalism. There is no wind of change that threatens the existing social order. Even in parts of South America, where the Bolivarian assault on global capitalism and its priorities has been the strongest, no systemic break has occurred. There is no major capitalist or hybrid state

---

2   The coinage is that of Adam Smith, who argued in *The Wealth of Nations* that China was such a paralysed state that it could not move forward or backward: 'China seems to have been long stationary, and had possibly long ago acquired that full complement of riches which is consistent with the nature of its laws and institutions', and 'inferior to what, with other laws and institutions, the nature of its soil and climate, and situation might admit of' (I.ix.15). The phrase might just as accurately describe the United States.

that even wishes to challenge US global power: China, Russia, leave alone the servile European Union, may have their quibbles, but even serious disputes (Ukraine, South China Sea) within the capitalist family of nation states seem far from developing into any frontal political challenge, or military confrontation, with Washington.[3]

This being the case, is there a convincing alternative explanation of the global struggle being waged by the United States today, other than to maintain mastery of the world? How else to explain the fact that, absent any rival imperialist contender, defence spending from 2006–2011 accounted for $2.75 trillion, and we are informed that the next five-year war plan (2013–2017) will require at least $2.7 trillion to fulfil?

Today there is no deep ideological and economic conflict on a level comparable to the struggle with Communism during the twentieth century. Over a span of more than seventy years, a series of grave conflicts were played out between capital and labour, parties and powers, institutions and masses; even more serious were the wars between states, the occupation of countries, the colonialisms of one kind or another (local military

---

3   This has never happened, not even during the Cold War period when there was more space available. Suggestions by left-wing writers (Ernest Mandel, Jon Halliday) in the sixties and seventies that Europe or Japan would emerge as rival imperialisms were sharply rebutted by history.

dictatorships the preferred variant) and the struggles against them. Each of these events had a profound impact on the political psychology of citizens and masters.

As the twenty-first century dawned, capitalist states, with national variations, dominated 99 per cent of the globe. The Communist enemy had been defeated. The spectre that haunted the world had been exorcised forever. This planetary triumph caused many to turn away from the past, from the nightmares but also the utopian face of history. A combination of nihilism – often the result of destroyed hopes and certainties – and self-deception overcame many critical citizens in the West. Some became passive spectators or active supporters of the new world order, busy reinventing themselves and rewriting their personal histories, caricaturing the radical upheavals of the past in which some had been enthusiastic participants. The resurgent popularity of religion and royalty, the explosion of consumerism and celebrity-worship, profit and pornography, cannot be completely dissociated from this turn.

The more engaged sections of the population looked forward to the 'peace dividend', 'democracy', 'human rights', and the spread of 'trickle-down' wealth. They thought that if US military and ideological domination was necessary to ensure all this, so much the better. But the much-anticipated golden age remained illusory. Imperial wars and capitalist greed dominated the political landscape. The 'war on terror' has been computed as costing $2,000 billion, twice the price of the Vietnam War. Confusion and apathy reign supreme as many a fettered nation in Europe and Africa – its ruling elites mired in corruptions of every sort – sinks closer to the abyss.

The new 'enemies' are either former Islamist allies, or new economic partners/rivals who refuse to surrender their sovereignty altogether. Ironically, this recalcitrance is fuelled by the very changes wrought by the new world order. If, for most of the preceding century, US military power and economic strength were interdependent, today the transformation of the globe by a tooth-and-claw capitalism has shifted the centre of the world market eastwards. Hence the obsession with China, the refusal to tolerate any notion of Japan as a sovereign state, and the disruption of attempts to unify the Korean Peninsula.

None of this was foreseen in the calculations of Zbigniew Brzezinski when he mapped the forward march of the United States in *The Grand Chessboard*.[4] Contrary to the advice of fellow-liberals and even some hard-headed conservatives, who hesitated to humiliate the defeated Soviet Union for fear of incubating revanchism, the leading realist strategist of the Democrats convinced Bill Clinton that nothing should be left to chance.

NATO had to expand and surround Russia. This was done with the agreement of the new elites in Moscow and

4   Zbigniew Brzezinski, *The Grand Chessboard: American Primacy and Its Geostrategic Imperatives* (New York, 1997).

St Petersburg, under the inebriated and corrupt leadership of Boris Yeltsin. When some of the more naïve Russian collaborators, only too happy to serve the interests of their new friends, suggested Russia join NATO and the EU, they were brutally snubbed. As far as the Euro-American ruling elites were concerned, the new Russia was simply too large to be properly digested. It was offered a bone in the shape of Chechnya. The West supported the razing of Grozny in the name of the 'war on terror'. It did not prove enough.[5]

The reassertion of Russian sovereignty and the rise of Vladimir Putin were the inevitable result of this tactic, albeit too late to prevent the dismemberment of Yugoslavia. Europe, viewed by Brzezinski as 'America's essential geopolitical bridgehead on the Eurasian continent', was more important than Japan since it 'entrenches American military power and political influence directly on the Eurasian mainland'.[6]

Nor was the blunt cold warrior of yesteryear reluctant to point out the new realities in this crucial region, using language similar to that of Clinton's successor, the much-reviled George W. Bush: 'The brutal fact is that Western

5   For an excellent study of how the Chechens and their country were treated, see Tony Wood, *Chechnya: The Case for Independence* (London and New York, 2007). The green-lighting of the massacres by the EU was in sharp contrast to the insistence on the freedom of the Baltic republics.

6   Brzezinski, *The Grand Chessboard*, p. 59.

Europe, and increasingly also Central Europe, remains largely an American protectorate, with its allied states reminiscent of ancient vassals and tributaries.' Britain was so servile that it barely counted. Germany and France were important, and in any division between these two, the Germans should be supported.

Brzezinski needn't have worried. Under Jospin and Sarkozy the French Republic happily embraced the Washington Consensus, with French mediatic intellectuals proving even more willing than their German equivalents.[7] There are no signs whatsoever of François Hollande breaking with this pattern, and in the unlikely event of a Red–Green victory at the next German elections, it would produce a government far closer to Washington than that of Angela Merkel. Since the collapse of the Berlin Wall, the European ruling class has never regarded continental independence, in the proper sense of the word, as a serious option.

Brzezinski's triumphalist celebration had noted that 'America stands supreme in the four decisive domains of global power.' Militarily, it was so far ahead of every other state as to be unchallengeable; economically, it was the indispensable motor of world growth; technologically, it led the innovation that was transforming the world; culturally, its appeal now stretched from Paris to Beijing and

---

7   In mapping the European present, Perry Anderson's essays have no contemporary equivalent. See in particular *The New Old World*.

seduced the new generations everywhere. The result: a hegemony without precedent in world history.

But the extent of its domination was not based on territorial control. In order to preserve its power the ruling elite needed to maintain a constant vigilance and a creative imagination. A decade and a half later, it is apparent that not all of Brzezinski's conditions for ensuring global supremacy are still in play. The financial crash of 2008 plunged Euro-America into a deep crisis, aggravated by the refusal of the rulers to contemplate an ameliorative new course for capitalism. The US economy, once the locomotive of the system, had become its guards' van.

The rise of a *sui generis* capitalism in China, a landmark geo-economic development by any measure, had, long before the 2008 crisis, transformed the United States into a debtor nation. This may well produce further surprises, but there is no evidence to suggest that these will include the propulsion of China towards proto-imperial status with its own co-prosperity sphere, defended by naval and air power and leading to its own occupations and colonizations.

For centuries the Chinese have relied on geography, logistics and manpower to transcend their backwardness in weaponry and have suffered as a result, especially at the hands of the Japanese. Were they to attempt to defend trade with arms today, it would necessitate a massive increase in military spending. Any such scenario would be strongly resisted at home by the elite. They well know how the Soviet Union imploded, and are also aware of the huge risks in provoking the United States militarily.

Until now China has shown little desire to challenge the United States politically, let alone militarily. Even those Chinese academics who urge a slightly tougher policy vis-à-vis Washington avoid suggesting military competition. Yan Xuetong of Tsinghua University appears to believe that Chinese global hegemony can best be established by taking measures for social justice at home. This Chinese 'hawk' argues that political power grows out of the heads of antique philosophers. A new-old humanism, based on ancient Chinese thought:

> According to the ancient Chinese philosopher Xunzi, there were three types of leadership: humane authority, hegemony and tyranny. Humane authority won the hearts and minds of the people at home and abroad. Tyranny – based on military force – inevitably created enemies. Hegemonic powers lay in between: they did not cheat the people at home or cheat allies abroad. But they were frequently indifferent to moral concerns and often used violence against non-allies. The philosophers generally agreed that humane authority would win in any competition with hegemony or tyranny.[8]

---

8   Yan Xuetong, 'How China Can Defeat America', *New York Times*, 20 November 2011.

Nevertheless, many non-Chinese thinkers believe that a struggle for world mastery by the Chinese against its global rivals is only a matter of time. They appear to be convinced by the scale of the recent economic convulsions that US hegemony has gone into irreversible decline.

Such pronouncements give economic determinism a bad name. The crash of 2008 had already been preceded by a long period of decline. For thirty years before-hand, the statistics were indicating economic and social failures: the richest country in the world could not ade-quately feed, employ or care for its poor, mainly African Americans and Hispanics. As Mike Davis wrote in 1984: 'A generation after the first "March on Washington" for jobs and freedom, black unemployment remains double that of whites, while black poverty is three times more common. Sixty per cent of employed black males (and 50 per cent of Hispanics) are concentrated in the spectrum of lowest-paid jobs.'[9]

For their part the US political–military elites believe that history is now firmly within their grasp for eternity, and were it to stray, military power can be effectively deployed to bring it back on course, as exemplified by the cruel wars of the late twentieth and twenty-first century. Imperial domination is based on technological superior-ity (especially in the military sphere), size and geography. Despite its weakened economic status, the United States

9   Mike Davis, 'The Political Economy of Late-Imperial America', *New Left Review*, January–February 1984.

remains infinitely more powerful than any other political entity in the world. The brazen use of this power continues to be visible on every continent. This is the determining factor in world politics today.[10]

Of course, serious problems persist. Social and hierarchical divisions in the populations of most countries are now so deeply embedded that, short of uprisings or revolutions, it is difficult to visualize any real transformation of class inequalities within the current system. When capitalist democracy hampers the functioning of capitalists, it is democracy that is truncated. In fact, as we shall see later in this chapter, capitalism functions best without democracy. Social, economic and political conditions will get worse, but on their own will pose no terminal threat to the system. Capitalism will not disappear of its own accord, and unless challenged it will remain averse to serious reforms that improve conditions for the majority.

Take, for example, the latest crisis: the 2008 crash that welcomed the Democrats into the White House. Seven years later, the new Depression shows few signs of recovery. Main Street remains Misery Street, while the systemic 'financial globalization' pioneered by Wall Street and

---

10 In *The Changing Face of Empire* (Chicago, 2012), Nick Turse provides an extremely useful geopolitical military map of the US presence in different parts of the world and charts the latest in military technology, including cyberwarfare, utilized to preserve hegemony.

which led to the collapse in the first instance still remains in place, buttressed by interventionist states.

In the old heartlands of Capital, such painful experiences – mass layoffs, rampant youth unemployment, dispossessions and repossessions – are relatively new for the twenty-first-century generation. They include being doused with the crocodile tears of the political–financial elites, who preach austerity for everyone except themselves. Meanwhile the media denounces, in sometimes hysterical tones, any alternative that challenges the status quo, however mildly.

The worship of money and private property remains the determining principle of world politics and culture. Despite a few flutters, the curtain is not going to come down on this epoch in a hurry. And state protection of the majority of citizens against the excesses of capitalism has virtually disappeared. Karl Polanyi's dream, in *The Great Transformation*, of social democracy as a universal panacea seems as remote today as the utopian section of the *Communist Manifesto*.[11]

Polanyi's warnings, however, were prescient. Stripped of all protection, 'human beings would perish from the effects of social exposure, they would die as victims of acute social dislocation'. Left unchecked, the capitalist nuclear-powered roller crushes all: 'nature would be reduced to its elements, neighbourhoods and landscapes

11   Karl Polanyi, *The Great Transformation: The Political and Economic Origins of Our Time* (second edition, New York, 2002).

defiled, military safety jeopardized, the power to produce food and raw materials destroyed.'

We're getting there. Most of sub-Saharan Africa, parts of South Asia, China, Brazil and Russia, together with the universal plight of migrants, provide the tragic confirmation. Meanwhile the greed of unfettered capital creates 'shortages and surfeits of money that would give rise to conditions as disastrous to business as floods and droughts in primitive society'. Polanyi's error was to imagine that regulated, social democratic capitalism was the normal, rational side of the system that could simply do with further strengthening.

Who can blame him for not foreseeing an implosion of the Soviet Union that also made social democracy redundant, to the delight of those who wanted a capitalism freed from every regulatory shackle so that it could rape the public sector as it pleased?

The citizens of Euro-America are confronted from cradle to grave with the crude idea that only what exists is possible. The system depersonalizes the individual economically, while stressing personal autonomy: the right to shop and the right to fornicate with a partner of one's choice. Of these the first is under threat because of the economic depression, while the second remains a front line of cultural warfare in North America and Europe.[12]

---

12   If the Turkish government, I once half-joked to a friend in Istanbul, legalized gay marriage, Turkey's chances of entering the hallowed European Union would triple overnight.

The individualism symbolized by the globe's latest billionaires tells its own illustrated tale: the kitsch mansions of the Russian oligarchs in Britain and Montenegro; the grotesque living quarters constructed by India's most celebrated tycoon in Bombay; the properties bought with their newly amassed fortunes by China's princelings, a hereditary caste without compare. And each palace filled with objects whose value is determined exclusively by the cost.

Rich Chinese, Indians and Russians desperately mimic the socio-economic architecture of old capitalism, as if the display of wealth was the real meaning of history. In Brazil, fortunes that could house many poor, landless peasant families are spent on an individual's cosmetic surgery, as another way of flaunting wealth. Alas, in these great times, for the dearth of the savage derision that once castigated the powerful: the likes of Juvenal, Martial and Petronius, the Popes, Byrons and Shelleys whose pens satirized the abuses of their day.[13] Conform or suffer is the motto of our rulers now.

Capitalism was once considered the epitome of economic evil, to such an extent that until recently the very word was avoided by its practitioners or apologists; it was the system that dared not speak its name. 'Freedom'

---

13 Among the few exceptions is the late Abdelrahman Munif, who in a set of brilliant novels savaged the rise of the oil dynasty in Saudi Arabia. We look forward to a Russian or Chinese or Euro-American equivalent.

was the preferred euphemism during most of the twentieth century. No longer. Capitalism has outed itself and, despite its troubles, is now lauded by banker and politician, portentous pundit and airhead breakfast TV host alike, on the grounds that no alternative is or ever could be desirable.

Therefore the least departure from capitalist norms on any continent, however moderately expressed or practised, arouses the frenzy of the privileged and their retinues. Fear of the unexpected – uprisings, electoral revolts that challenge the status quo, street protests by the young, peasant jacqueries – compels the global elites to depend, in the last instance, on the threat or use of US military strength to settle every dispute in their favour. This creates a level playing field for the global rich alone, regardless of the resulting slaughter. Baghdad, Helmand, Tripoli, Kinshasa tell the tale.

Not since the interwar years has conflict been incited so shamelessly, and with such frightening frivolity. The combination of unchallengeable military power and the political intoxication it produces sweeps all else to the side. What the whole world knows to be false is proclaimed by the United States to be the truth, with media networks, vassals and acolytes obediently in tow. The triumph of crude force is portrayed as a mark of intelligence or courage; criminal arrogance is described as moral energy. Of course, such aggression doesn't always succeed politically and, in most cases, the chaos it unleashes is much worse than what existed before. But the economic gains are palpable: the privatization of Libyan and Iraqi oil are the most salient examples.

How can hope be sustained in such a world? First, by shedding all illusions about the capacity of the rulers of the world to reform themselves. The conditions and circumstances that have enabled US imperial power to reach its present level of ascendancy are hardly a secret. And the questions currently being debated are extremely relevant. What are the limits of US power? What factors might contribute to its decline? How is US hegemony exercised today? The answers would take into account America's size, natural resources, technology, manpower and military superiority, compared to those of its economic rivals, and also consider how long domestic consent to such an existence is liable to continue.

A well-meaning, if obvious, short cut is to indulge in wishful thinking, which comes in various guises. The simplest of these queries the very notion of an imperial United States of America, especially after the collapse of the Soviet Union. Some write of the differences between the old European pattern of colonization and the current variant, employing a sleight of mind to give Washington a clean bill of health. Such a view ignores institutions and emphasizes individuals. To present the aggressive post-9/11 forward march as the initiative of 'crazies' (Cheney/Rumsfeld), or a dumb and malign George W. Bush, encourages amnesia.

The fact that Obama/Clinton have effectively continued the policies of the preceding administration and, in
some cases, gone beyond them suggests that Bush and his
associates did not have a monopoly on 'craziness'.[14]

The political literature on the decline and coming fall
of the American Empire has proliferated in recent years,
and is equally unsatisfactory. There is an air of despera-
tion. Setbacks are interpreted as crushing defeats, while
deluded hopes fasten onto the rise of China, or Putin's
Russia, or even onto political Islam.[15] In reality, the
imperial highway is unconquered and unconquerable
from without; the only serious exit route lies within the
country. What combination of social forces at home can
defeat the labyrinthine power structures of the United
States? However bleak such a vision might appear at the
moment, there is no other on the horizon.

A 'good' patriot today is made to feel that she must, of
necessity, also be pro-imperialist. More sceptical citizens
who believe that the Empire's military bases should be
dismantled, its troops brought home, its military expenditure reduced, and America itself redefined as just a large

---

14   Even an astute historian like Eric Hobsbawm could write:
'Frankly, I can't make sense of what has happened in the United
States since 9/11 that enabled a group of political crazies to realize
long-held plans for an unaccompanied solo performance of world
supremacy.' *On Empire* (New York, 2008), p. 57.

15   Emmanuel Todd's *After the Empire: The Breakdown of the
American Order* (New York, 2006) is a case in point.

state among others, only using force when it is directly threatened, are viewed as 'bad' patriots, which is to say, little more than back-stabbing traitors.[16] They are by default the enemy within.

They are regarded as such not only at home, but also by those who fear US withdrawal abroad: vassal politicians and states in Europe, Asia, the Middle East, Africa, and the loyal few in South America. The rulers of the only vassal continent – Australia – would, given its geography, be equally disturbed to contemplate independence.

Yet in both the Arab world and the heartlands of Western capitalism, the systemic order imposed through the Washington Consensus since the collapse of the Soviet Union has appeared to be in forward flight. The Arab world seeks to escape its recent history, while some European states, in the grip of parliamentary paralysis, dream of external deliverance from the very bankers who were responsible for the crash of 2008. The atrophy of the productive economy in the United States and large swathes of the EU reveal a malady that was already at an advanced stage, even as some claimed that the disease had been defeated forever. In response, the optimists argued that the US was confronted by an involution similar to the one that had afflicted Britain at the heyday of its empire. Questions long treated as defunct began to be raised again, if only on the margins of the political system.

16   John Mearsheimer, the late Chalmers Johnson, Andrew Bacevich, Noam Chomsky, to name a few.

The impact of this doubt on popular consciousness has spread rapidly. The events have laid bare the weaknesses of the system, exposed its bald patches, and revealed yet again that the motive force underlying empires, wars and conquest for the last two thousand years is not ideology, but the drive to accumulate and monopolize the distribution and flow of wealth by all necessary means. The struggle to extract and transport gold and silver may have been replaced by split-second, push-button transfers on tiny machines, like the Thompson gun has been replaced by the drone, but the masters of our world are playing the same ruthless game as their forebears.

The year 2011 witnessed the concatenation of two crises. One was symbolized by the spate of Arab uprisings challenging indigenous and Western-backed despotisms in the name of freedom. These events were much more reminiscent of the 1848 upheavals in continental Europe than of the 'springtime of the peoples' of 1989, which effectively exchanged one form of dependence for another, seeing in neoliberal capitalism the only future.

The other blew in like a breeze through public spaces and university campuses once again, and the noise of mass uproar could be heard on more than one continent. Mediterranean Europe in particular was engulfed by general strikes and mass mobilizations numbering millions. Do these disruptions herald the birth of a new social order, inside or outside capitalism?

The answer from the upper classes is a resounding

'No'. They have been hard at work using the state to bail out (Europe) or stimulate (US) the existing neoliberal system. The notion that there might be a managerial revolt from within the system, a technocrats' uprising, belongs to the realm of science-fiction. It has no precedent in history. Any change from above or within the existing structures is unlikely, unless the threats from below become too strong to resist.

Over the course of 2011–2012, the continuing economic story was the severe crisis of the Wall Street system: the failure of the attempt to sustain profits in Euro-America and Japan through an over-reliance on fictitious capital, and the collapse of various European economies – Iceland, Ireland, Greece, Spain, Portugal and Italy – kept together by Euro-sticking plaster.

The major difference between this latest systemic crisis and its 1929 forebear is not related so much to the exact nature of the crisis. Then, the financial sector was flanked by cartels and professionally managed corporations (separating ownership from the onerous tasks of daily admin), created in response to the 1890 crisis. In the thirty years that followed, a frenetic process of financialization took place, led by an unregulated top layer of capitalists as well as by shabby hucksters turned multi-millionaires thanks to the huge, untaxed profits of criminal enterprise. Aided by equally unscrupulous managers, all were engaged in unbridled speculation, orgies of profit-enhancement on a hitherto unimaginable scale.

It was this that triggered the crash of 1929 and the Great Depression.[17]

The magnitude of the crisis on its own did not lead to palliatives. It was an unusual combination of external and domestic factors that helped reform the system. These were: the existence of the Soviet Union (still seen at the time by millions across the globe as a viable anti-capitalist alternative), the growing polarization between fascism and the parties of the left in Europe, and the radicalization and unionization of American labour (which reached a peak with the workers' occupation of the motor plants in Flint, Michigan in 1936, creating a new mood for change).

These were the factors that delivered a set of Keynesian, social democratic reforms. The popularity of this outcome can be judged by the three successive terms awarded to the New Deal president Franklin Roosevelt. Greatly helped by the war economy, the system created and sustained a long postwar boom that enabled rising wages, full employment and the welfare state.

This boom ended in 1970. The series of defeats inflicted on the US and Western European labour movements in the decade that followed were the prelude to the era of neoliberal globalization. This was followed by the collapse of the Soviet Union and the decision of

17   Gérard Duménil and Dominique Lévy, veteran scholars at the state-funded Centre national de recherche scientifique in Paris, have written what is probably the best comparative study of the 1929 and 2008 crises: *The Crisis of Neo-Liberalism* (Harvard, 2011).

the capitalist-roaders in the Chinese politburo to take another great leap forward. The tectonic plates had moved. Everywhere the level of economic inequality has rapidly increased, with social rights eroded and political rights overridden. The corporate mass media defend the interests of capital, while the politicians are permanently in hock to both. The miseries of the less privileged rarely encroach on the bubble of the rich.

Despite the depth of the crisis, the capitalist universe was in a state of petrified immobility. Incapable of dumping the neoliberal albatross overboard, it carried on in the same old way as banking scandals continued to erupt. The tremors of dislocation affected every continent, but the United States and its European allies held firm. What gave them the strength to cling to this particular breed of capitalism was the fact that, barring a few republics in South America practising a left-variant of social democracy with majority popular support, no alternative emerged on the political horizon. Predatory capitalists and predatory politicians continued to rule the roost.[18]

The neoliberal system has been dented by the crash of 2008, but there has been no irretrievable breakdown. It is premature to imagine that capitalism is on the verge of dissolution; however, its political cover is a different story. The democratic shell within which Western capitalism

18   Peter Mair's *Ruling the Void* is an eloquent, disturbing study of the course of democratic decline over the last three decades.

has, until recently, prospered is showing a number of cracks. Since the nineties democracy has, in the West, taken the form of an extreme centre, in which centre-left and centre-right collude to preserve the status quo; a dictatorship of capital that has reduced political parties to the status of the living dead. How did we get here?

Following the collapse of Communism in 1991, Edmund Burke's notion that 'in all societies consisting of different classes, certain classes must necessarily be uppermost', and that 'the apostles of equality only change and pervert the natural order of things', became the wisdom of the age, embraced by servant and master alike. Nevertheless, money corrupted politics. Leading politicians of the extreme centre became rich during their years in power. Many were given consultancies as soon as they left office, as part of a 'sweetheart deal' with the companies concerned.

Throughout the heartlands of capital we have witnessed the convergence of political choices: Republicans and Democrats in the United States, New Labour and Tories in Britain, Socialists and Conservatives in France; the German coalitions, the Scandinavian centre-right and centre-left, and so on. In virtually each case the two-party system has morphed into an effective national government. The hallowed notion that political parties and the differences between them constitute the essence of modern democracies has begun to look like a sham.

Cultural differences persist, and the issues raised are important; but the craven capitulation on the fundamentals of how the country is governed means that cultural liberals, in permanent hock to the US Democrats or their equivalents, have helped to create the climate in which so many social and cultural rights are menaced.

A new market extremism has come into play. The symbiosis between politics and corporate capital has become a model for the new-style democracies. It was the politicians who ushered private capital into the most sacred domains of social provision.

The rape of the public sector was regarded as a necessary 'reform'. Private finance initiatives were touted as the best way to fund essential services, despite warnings that this would reduce the latter to indentured slave status, in permanent debt. But this became the norm. Countries such as France and Germany, accused of dragging their feet on the way to the neoliberal paradise, were regularly denounced in the English-language press. Today the full cost of this folly is clearly visible.[19]

---

19   The *Guardian*'s lead story on 5 July 2012 exposed the scale of the disaster that had been pushed through by successive Labour Governments: 'The 717 PFI contracts currently under way across the UK are funding new schools, hospitals and other public facilities with a total capital value of £54.7 billion, but the overall ultimate cost will reach £301 billion by the time they have been paid off over the coming decades. Much of this difference is due to ongoing running costs built into the contracts, but the schemes have also been criticised

To question this turn, to defend the public sector, to advocate the state ownership of utilities, to challenge the fire sale of public housing, was to be regarded, during the first stage of this process, as a 'conservative' dinosaur, and more lately as a subversive, threatening to disrupt the cosy consensus. Indeed, the language of the new capitalist order deserves a study to itself, modelled on Klemperer's brilliant work on how the language was altered and subverted during the Third Reich to such an extent that even staunch anti-fascists began to use some words without thinking.[20]

As 2014 drew to a close, how did the United States fare? Far from appearing overstretched or on the verge of collapse, America was conducting business as usual across the world. The NATO intervention and 'victory' in Libya was carried out via a monopoly of air space, sealing Africa Command's first military triumph, setting the tone for

for providing poor value for money compared with the interest rates the government would pay if it borrowed money directly to pay for the schemes. Last week, South London Healthcare Trust, which runs three hospitals in south-east London, was placed in administration by the health secretary as it struggled to meet the cost of its PFI obligations. Dave Prentis, general secretary of the union Unison, said on Thursday night: "The NHS is just the start of the story." We're sitting on a PFI debt time bomb, and the sheer scale of the burden paints a seriously grim picture for the future of our public services.'

20   Victor Klemperer, *Language of the Third Reich: LTI: Lingua Tertii Imperii* (London, 2013).

dealing with the rest of the continent in the decade that lies ahead. The Arab East remains unstable; nevertheless, the moderate Islamist forces in the region are only too happy to accommodate most imperial needs, with the odd disagreement on Israel largely for show and not reflecting any fundamental shift in policy. The Taliban and ISIS will do the same when the time comes. Meanwhile, the oil giants – BP, Chevron, ExxonMobil, Shell and Conoco-Phillips – netted profits in the region of $900 billion over the last decade.

As David Vine points out in a recent essay, all Obama's pieties regarding intra-Muslim violence in the Middle East ignore the fact that his own policies, as well as those of the arms industry, have nurtured these rivalries and related conflicts:

Since mid-year [2014], for example, the State Department and the Pentagon have helped pave the way for the United Arab Emirates (UAE) to buy hundreds of millions of dollars' worth of High Mobility Artillery Rocket Systems (HIMARS), launchers and associated equipment and to spend billions more on Mine Resistant Ambush Protected (MRAP) vehicles; for Lebanon to purchase nearly $200 million in Huey helicopters and supporting gear; for Turkey to buy hundreds of millions of dollars of AIM-120C-7 AMRAAM (air-to-air) missiles, and for Israel to stock up on half a billion dollars' worth of AIM-9X Sidewinder (air-to-air) missiles; not to mention other deals to aid the militaries of Egypt, Kuwait, and Saudi Arabia.

> For all the news coverage of the Middle East, you rarely see significant journalistic attention given to any of this or to agreements like the almost $70 million contract, signed in September, that will send Hellfire missiles to Iraq, Jordan, Saudi Arabia, and Qatar, or the $48 million Navy deal inked that same month for construction projects in Bahrain and the UAE.[21]

Elsewhere further advances are dotted on the world map. The traditionally servile Australian elite agreed to a new US military base in Australia with alacrity. This was accompanied by hard anti-Chinese talk in which President Obama underlined the imperial presence in the Far East, stressing that the US was an Asian power and warning the Chinese to 'play by the rules of the road'. These are rules that the Chinese know are formulated, interpreted and enforced by the US.

Elsewhere, only South America has experienced a rise of political resistance to imperial hegemony, both political and economic. This is the first time since the Monroe Doctrine that four states are without US ambassadors: Cuba, Venezuela, Ecuador and Bolivia. The largest state in the region, Brazil, has asserted a degree of independence lacking in recent decades. State Department functionaries visit Brasilia regularly to reassure the political elite that 'Obama is not Bush', a message greeted with some scepticism.

---

21 David Vine, 'A Permanent Infrastructure for Permanent War', 13 November 2014, TomDispatch.com.

It is hardly a secret that Obama/Clinton approved the coup in Honduras and that death squads are back in favour. Plans to destabilize the Bolivarian states and topple their governments have not been abandoned, as the 2012 overthrow of Fernando Lugo in Paraguay revealed. Washington searches out the weakest link in the enemy camp and then proceeds to destroy it, with military force when necessary, but preferably by using local relays and manipulating the system, as in Asunción, and in Venezuela after Chávez succumbed to cancer.

To think that the military-political leadership of the United States is preparing to go back home after organizing a soft dismantling of its overseas empire is eminently comforting and wholly untrue.

The economic situation in the US and Europe is serious, but not terminal. The economic, political and military components of the present crisis are the direct result of the capitalist triumphalism that gripped the West after the fall of the Berlin Wall in 1989. The strategic and economic policies prescribed by the United States and accepted without question by their global allies – the Washington Consensus – were not hasty improvisations. The gleeful governors of the new world order, initially surprised by the speed of the collapse in the Soviet Union, moved rapidly to take full advantage of circumstances.

The dawn of the 'unipolar moment' was seen in the *blitzkrieg* of the 1991 Gulf War, which sealed American pre-eminence and exorcized the ghosts of Vietnam. For a brief period American hegemony appeared complete. But the absence of a global rival, NATO's 'humanitarian' interventions of the nineties and the so-called Revolution in Military Affairs (RMA) paved the way for the wars fought in the occupied world of Islam – Iraq, Afghanistan and Libya. The huge advantage in all these conflicts was the unchallenged command of the skies, but that alone is never sufficient to ensure permanent gain. Even on its own terms, the military-technological revolution that boasts of a capacity for deadly precision strikes based on 'first-rate' intelligence and embedded media support has not been an unmitigated success, a fact most clearly visible in the Af-Pak zone of operations.

Following the humiliation in Vietnam, a chastened US military was wary of the piecemeal use of force for resolving political problems. Reforms under Marine General Creighton Abrams and later Defense Secretary Caspar Weinberger had tried to place checks on the easy recourse to force by politicians. The Weinberger Doctrine – which subsequently evolved into the Powell Doctrine – prioritized diplomacy without ruling out force. Indeed, it prescribed 'overwhelming force'; but only after all diplomatic options had been exhausted and an exit strategy laid out.

This policy divided the military hierarchy from the neoconservatives, who have always favoured pre-emption. In 1991 when Iraq invaded Kuwait, Bush, Powell, and Baker were all reluctant at first to intervene.

The initial cheerleaders were Scowcroft and Cheney, and the latter's neoconservative retinue. The war proved to be a successful test case for the Powell Doctrine; it also rehabilitated war as a tool of statecraft. Round-the-clock television coverage which focused on the dazzling display of hi-tech weaponry while excluding the victims made war seem palatable, even exciting.

From its success in the Gulf, the military came away with the expectation that in future it would only participate in large-scale conventional warfare consistent with the Powell Doctrine. To maintain a qualitative edge, the military brass undertook to maintain sufficient forces to fight and win two major wars concurrently; the costs of maintaining this capacity ballooned. The availability of such awesome military power and the absence of a rival soon spurred liberal interventionists in the Clinton administration to consider limited displays of American power for philanthropic purposes, despite the military's reluctance.

Under Madeleine Albright US policy grew progressively more interventionist, and the check that the Powell Doctrine was supposed to be found itself ultimately undercut by Powell's unbridled enthusiasm for strengthening the military. The limited, 'humanitarian' interventions of the nineties helped bury the Powell Doctrine as well as the sanctity of state sovereignty enshrined in the Westphalian system and the UN Charter. From the invasion of Panama in 1989 to the invasion of Iraq in 2003, the United States would participate in nine major campaigns. A blue-ribbon commission appointed by the US government in 1999 reported that 'since the end of the Cold War, the United States has embarked upon nearly four dozen military interventions ... as opposed to only sixteen during the entire period of the Cold War.'

The Iraq and Afghanistan wars in particular have strained the military, to a degree that prompted Colin Powell to pronounce it 'broken'. However, the real reckoning has been postponed by the fact that the wars have been waged largely on credit, and the real costs have yet to come due. Much was made of the fact to wage the First Gulf War, the US spent a (by recent comparison) paltry $61.1 billion, of which $36 billion was borrowed from the Saudis, Kuwaitis and other Gulf States, and $16 billion from Germany and Japan.

In addition, the US has since spent $4.3 billion a year in compensation, pension, and disability benefits to the more than 200,000 veterans of the war. This, as Joseph Stiglitz and Linda Bilmes note, does not even scratch the surface of the real costs from the lost income of the nearly 100,000 soldiers suffering from Gulf War syndrome, 40,000 of whom also have long-term disabilities. The proportion of veterans claiming disability benefits in the global war on terror is much higher, but Stiglitz and Bilmes estimate that even in the best-case scenario, three-quarters of a million veterans will eventually claim disability benefits at a cost of $688 billion.

The government routinely downplays the actual costs of the war; but more importantly, even if one takes account of the full budgetary costs (which they estimate at $2.7 trillion by 2008) one would still fail to get a clear picture of the total economic costs ($5 trillion). According to estimates in 2011, the US would be spending 10 per cent of its total Federal Budget on interest payments alone, mainly as a result of the high borrowing to finance the war. The servicing of the debt from both wars will eventually come to a realistic estimate of $816 billion. As Stiglitz and Bilmes write,

> A trillion dollars could have built 8 million additional housing units, could have hired some 15 million additional public school teachers for one year; could have paid for 120 million children to attend a year of Head Start; or insured 530 million children for health care for one year; or provided 43 million students with four-year scholarships at public universities.[22]

For the foreseeable future the United States will remain the world's preeminent military power. While there may be states that can field larger armies, the US maintains a qualitative edge in air and naval power. With eleven naval task forces organized around ten Nimitz-class and one Enterprise-class nuclear-powered aircraft carriers, the US capacity for power projection remains unmatched. It also operates the most extensive network of bases.

22   Joseph Stiglitz and Linda Bilmes, *The Three Trillion Dollar War* (New York, 2008), p. xv.

According to the Pentagon's Base Structure Report for Fiscal Year 2010, the US had 662 bases overseas and another eighty-eight in US Territories (overseas possessions such as the Pacific Islands), concentrated in strategic locations such as Central Europe, the Middle East, Asia-Pacific, Latin America's Andean region, the Caribbean, and East and West Africa. The actual number is much larger, and fluctuates from year to year. The annual Base Structure Report excludes installations in combat zones such as Iraq and Afghanistan, and facilities leased in politically sensitive regions such as Israel, Pakistan or Qatar.

It also excludes the sprawling Camp Bondsteel in Ferizaj, Kosovo, which among other things has been accused of housing a Guantánamo-style CIA detention facility. An exact figure of the number of facilities the US operates worldwide is hard to come by, but if one adds to those listed the nearly 400 facilities in Afghanistan and the eighty-eight in Iraq (down from over 400), the total exceeds a thousand. Not all of these are on the scale of Bondsteel, however, and most, especially in combat zones, are temporary facilities (known as Forward Operating Bases).

Nevertheless, at home the age of military Keynesianism is over. During the Eisenhower era, the defence budget accounted for half of federal spending and 10 per cent of GDP, but unemployment was low and the US was a creditor nation. Today it is the world's most indebted nation and the unemployment rate has been running at 9.8 per cent. According to 2010 census figures, one in seven Americans is living below the poverty line. Meanwhile the US spends a million dollars annually to train, equip, and maintain a single soldier in Iraq or Afghanistan. It can't maintain this level of outgoings.

According to the Congressional Budget Office, the US federal deficit will reach a record $1.5 trillion in 2011. On 26 January 2011, CBO director Douglas Elmendorf announced,

> We estimate that if current laws remain unchanged, the budget deficit this year will be close to $1.5 trillion, or 9.8 percent of GDP. That would follow deficits of 10 percent of GDP and 8.9 percent of GDP in the past two years, the three largest deficits since 1945. As a result, debt held by the public will probably jump from 40 percent of GDP at the end of fiscal year 2008 to nearly 70 percent at the end of fiscal year 2011.

The single biggest factor was the tax deal between Obama and the Republican Party that extended the Bush-era tax cuts for the wealthiest Americans, cutting government revenues by nearly $400 billion. The US National Debt has already passed a record $14 trillion.

By comparison, China has emerged from the 2008 financial crisis with few bruises. It has maintained spectacular growth rates and in the second quarter of 2010, it overtook Japan as the world's second-largest economy (a position which Japan had maintained for nearly four decades). Valued at $1.33 trillion, its economy is already bigger than that of Germany, the UK or France. By the end of 2010 its foreign exchange reserves stood at $2.85 trillion. According to a 2009 Goldman Sachs report, it will also overtake the US economy by 2027 (and the BRIC countries, Brazil, Russia, India and China, are set to displace the G7 as the largest economic bloc by 2032).

When Admiral Timothy Keating, the head of US Pacific Command, met a senior Chinese admiral in the crisis year of 2008, he heard a surprising offer. Keating reported that his unnamed counterpart had suggested drawing a line down the middle of the Pacific, adding: 'You guys can have the east part of the Pacific: Hawaii to the States. We'll take the west part: Hawaii to China.' It was only a joke, but its timing was significant, touching as it did on what is likely to be the most sensitive and loaded topic in international politics over the next fifty years.

Between 2002 and 2008, the dollar steadily devalued under the burden of the balance of payments and the government deficit, losing 40 per cent of its value. The slide was briefly checked by the recession, but by March 2009 it had resumed. In an ominous move for the US, in 2009 China suggested that the dollar be phased out as the world's reserve currency, to be replaced by a basket of currencies. There is already a currency war underway with China, accused by the US – and to a lesser extent the EU – of keeping the renminbi artificially low to boost exports.

In 2011, as the crisis showed few signs of abating at home and with the interrelationship of the global economy on public display, Admiral Mike Mullen, the retiring chairman of the Joint Chiefs of Staff, declared that US debt was now the most serious threat to national security. With the 2011 budget deficit approaching a record-breaking $1,580 billion, his concern cannot be dismissed. He did not suggest a solution. Targeted raids on Wall Street and the US Treasury, or draining the Federal Reserve, wouldn't solve the problem here.

Will the US continue to be the dominant power in the Pacific and East Asia – or will it be supplanted by China? Although weaker economically than it has ever been over the last half-century, the United States has never been as strong militarily and ideologically as it is today. Despite the overstretch, all forecasts predicting the imminent downfall of the American Empire are a combination of economic determinism and wishful thinking.

In 2010, the Chinese economy was still slightly over a third the size of the US economy. But, unlike the heavily leveraged US economy, the Chinese economy is robust and dynamic. In 2009, China's GDP grew 8.7 per cent, whereas that of the United States fell 2.4 per cent. In 2007, China had $4.8 trillion in household and corporate savings, equivalent to 160 per cent of its GDP, a figure that is projected to reach $17.7 trillion by 2020. In 2001, the average Chinese household saved 25.3 per cent of disposable income; by comparison, an American house-hold saved only 6.4 per cent in 2002.

Though inequality remains a major issue, it is not as conspicuous as in Russia or India; in 2007, the Forbes richest 100 list didn't feature a single Chinese. Per capita income has risen from $339 in 1990 to over $1,000 in 2003, and is expected to double in the next ten years. The number of people living in poverty has fallen from 250 million in 1978 to 29.27 million in 2001, accounting for three-quarters of global poverty reduction in this period. Between 2001 and 2006 its overseas investments grew at the rate of 60 per cent, reaching $50 billion by 2008. Hitherto China has emphasized imitation over innovation, but in 2006, according to the OECD, China overtook Japan to become the world's largest R & D investor after the US.

China is no threat to the US, but it is a threat to US hegemony. With the exception of Japan and Taiwan, East Asia is now a Chinese sphere of influence. Even South Korea has been forging closer ties with China. Though Taiwanese nationalism remains robust, its economic reli-ance on China has been growing. The Chinese market absorbs 40 per cent of all of Taiwan's exports.

Much has also been made of China's growing mili-tary ambitions following the test flight of a prototype Chengdu J-20, a fifth-generation stealth fighter. How-ever, the aircraft is not slated to become operational until 2017–2019. And even a fleet of J-20s will only add to China's defensive capabilities, since it still lacks power projection capabilities. Though it operates the second-largest naval force after the US, its technology is mostly primitive, and as of February 2011, it still doesn't have a single aircraft carrier. By comparison the Indian Navy has been operating aircraft carriers since the 1970s, including the former HMS *Hermes*, of Falklands fame, and it can also fly its fleet of Sea Harrier jets off of the amphibious INS *Jalashwa*. Chinese Defence Minister Liang Guanglie himself has conceded that 'We cannot call ourselves an advanced military country. The gap between us and advanced countries is at least two to three decades.'

So far China's military posture is defensive, with an emphasis on deterrence. It has shown no aggressive intent, but from time to time it has asserted its capacity to defend its own sphere of influence. In response to US advances in Ballistic Missile Defense technology (known as 'Star Wars' or SDI under Reagan), in 2007 China demonstrated its ability to neutralize any offensive advantage which SDI might afford by successfully testing an anti-satellite missile to destroy one of its own satellites.

However, opinions differ as to whether China's rise will be peaceful or will lead to conflict. Opinions vary even among realists. John Mearsheimer argues that China's rise will not be peaceful. He bases his argument on the realist assumption that all great powers aim for hegemony in their own region and deny this to other powers. The international system for Mearsheimer is characterized by three factors:

1) states operate in anarchy with no higher power;
2) all great powers have offensive capability, or the capacity to hurt one another;
3) no state can know the intentions of other states, especially their future intentions.

States therefore fear one another, especially as there is no 999 to call. As a result they seek to maximize their power: great powers don't just aim to be the strongest, they aim to be hegemonic, that is, the only great power in the system.

For Mearsheimer, global hegemony is impossible in the modern system. Instead states aim to be regional hegemons in their own sphere, while denying others the same degree of dominance in theirs. In other words they don't want peer competitors; they like to keep other regions divided, so that they'll compete with one another and be unable to focus on them. This, at least, is how the US and other great powers have acted in the past.

On this assumption, Mearsheimer argues that China will try to maximize the power gap with regional rivals like Japan, Russia and India. It will also try to push the US out of its sphere of influence (as the US did with Europe in Latin America) and develop its own Monroe Doctrine. This will inevitably lead to conflict with the US, since it doesn't tolerate a peer competitor. The US will therefore go to any lengths to contain and weaken China. China's neighbours will also be worried about its rise, and might join forces with the US in a balancing coalition to contain it. The US and Japan will want to prevent Taiwan falling into Chinese hands and will seek to strengthen it, fuelling further competition between the US and China.

However, Mearsheimer's colleague, Stephen Walt, demurs from what he considers Mearsheimer's 'hard-core structuralist' predictions. He sees a 'slightly higher probability of a relatively benign outcome'. While conceding that 'the continued increase in Chinese economic power is virtually certain to lead to increased security competition between the United States and China', he argues that it is not certain

> just how intense or dangerous that security competition will ultimately become ... Because I put more weight on geography, on the offensive potential of deployed military power, and on perceived intentions, I see somewhat greater possibilities for keeping that future competition within bounds. In particular, a lot depends on the extent to which China develops large power-projection capabilities and begins to push for major changes in the East Asian status quo. Some movement in that direction is likely, I think, but the speed and intensity of these trends will determine how alarmed the United States and its allies become and how vigorously they respond.[23]

However, he notes, all of this presumes a reasonably sensible, prudent, and mature leadership in both countries.

---

23   Stephen Walt, 'Will Washington and Beijing Be Mature Enough to Cooperate', *Foreign Policy*, 13 August 2010.

But things could easily change if either country becomes led by fanatics.

For the Chinese International Relations scholar Yan Xuetong, the US–Chinese policy of maintaining an overt pretence of friendship is fraught with danger: it could easily lead to conflict, since neither side knows the other's red lines. He therefore suggests that to prevent triggering an unwanted conflict it is important for the two sides to agree that they are cultural friends, business partners, political competitors, and military adversaries.

There is a marked difference in the Chinese and American approaches to expansion. The US preference for power over diplomacy is highlighted in the stark disparity between the budgets of the State and Defense Departments. Whereas the US government has been spending over a trillion dollars annually since 2007, the combined budgets for the State Department and USAID for Fiscal Year 2010 was only $48.6 billion, despite a 7 per cent increase over Fiscal Year 2009 funding levels. Even the official budgets of the seventeen intelligence agencies are twice as large as that of the State Department.

To be sure, there have been occasional confrontations between the two powers – such as over the Taiwan Strait in 1995–96, over the bombing of the Chinese embassy in Belgrade in 1999, and the collision between a Chinese jet and an American spy plane in 2001 – but China has been careful to avoid showdowns.

Chinese military doctrine, according to Martin Jacques, is rooted in Sun Zi's writings: it sets much greater store on seeking to weaken and isolate the enemy than on actually fighting him. Thus China relies exclusively on trade to expand its influence. Despite its vast economic investments, it has yet to acquire a single foreign base (although it is investing in maritime facilities in Pakistan and Myanmar, in case trade routes in the South China Sea become blocked).

Many have argued that the US went to war in Afghanistan and Iraq to seize the region's energy resources, or to secure pipelines. However, the real beneficiary of both wars has been China. It has not only obtained some of the biggest contracts in Iraq, it recently also won a $3.4 billion contract – the largest in Afghan history – to mine copper in Logar province. (Adding insult to injury, Chinese investments in Afghanistan are now protected by American armed forces.)

Chinese and Indian companies also supplied all seven finalists in Afghanistan's second great mineral project, said to contain 60 billion tons of iron ore. China has invested far more in extracting Iraqi oil than American companies have, and ever since the US excluded itself from the Iranian market in the mid-1990s with the Iran and Libya Sanctions Act, China has made the most of the unrivalled access. It has recently reached long-term arrangements to buy gas from Iran. In 2007, China's top suppliers of oil were, in order of importance, Angola, Saudi Arabia,

Iran, Russia, Oman, Congo, Yemen, Equatorial Guinea and Venezuela.

Whereas the US has been primarily concerned with exploiting cheap labour and investing in oil and commodities, writes Jacques, 'the Chinese assistance usually comes in the form of a package, including infrastructural projects like roads, railways and major public buildings, as well as provision of technical expertise.' It also has fewer strings attached. In 2006, for example, the Chinese state-owned company CMEC 'swept the bidding for one of the world's largest known iron ore deposits, in Gabon, by offering to build a 360-mile railroad to the nearly inaccessible mine site, two hydroelectric dams to power the mine and a deepwater ocean port to export the mined ore'. This is how a commentator at the *New York Times* summarizes the situation:

> The United States views Southwest Asia mostly as a security threat. China sees it as an opportunity. Decades of military cooperation with Pakistan, which shares India as a rival, have flowered into an economic alliance. A Chinese-built deepwater port in Gwadar, Pakistan, on the Gulf of Oman, is expected eventually to carry Middle Eastern oil and gas over the western Himalayas into China.[24]

---

24 Michael Wines, 'China Willing to Spend Big on Afghan Commerce', *New York Times*, 29 December 2009.

It will not be easy for China to become a regional hegemon, implementing its version of the Monroe Doctrine. Whereas the US was surrounded mainly by weak states, China has powerful competitors in Japan, Russia and India, two of which are likely to band together with the US to contain a powerful China. China is more likely to rely on its economy to gain leverage over neighbouring powers, increasing their dependence.

Though China has hitherto been excluded from the G8, in 2008 the decline of the West's economic power was on display when even Bush had to turn to the G20 instead. China has already forged free trade agreements with ASEAN and has also joined a regional rival to the IMF. None of this necessitates a break with the United States, unless the latter embarks on some suicidal adventure on the Chinese mainland.

However irritating it may appear to some – and on all sides of the political spectrum – the fact remains that, despite the difficulties it confronts, the United States still embodies a strong and meaningful imperialism. Its hardest tests lie ahead. The danger inherent in the position it occupies is a natural consequence of ultra-imperialism: the concentration of global power in the hands of a single powerful state leads inexorably to world tyranny. Such a diagnosis may be unsettling, but is necessary for the development of long-term regional strategies for change.

And there is another question. Who will bring the mother ship down?

The course of a powerful empire cannot be diverted without huge political convulsions at home or a serious challenge from abroad. The former might result from wars, or an economic collapse on a huge scale that forces a retreat; the latter from the presence of a rival, skulking patiently in the wings.

The centre of the world market has shifted eastwards to China, as once it did westwards from Britain to the United States, but the engine of military power and its attendant civil institutions that protect and sustain the system of global capitalism remain firmly anchored in Washington. The Pacific and the Atlantic are both the setting for an outsize military-industrial complex and the world's largest national economy. The interrelationship between the two is likely to determine the course of the twenty-first century, with Europe remaining attached to the Atlantic.

7

Fear, Misery, Power and the Forty-Fifth US President

In 2008, in my book *The Obama Syndrome*, I described Barack Obama as the most inventive apparition of the American Empire. In polar contrast, the presidential election in 2016 produced Donald Trump, a nightmare for the imperial establishment, whose politburo is working overtime to bring the great Lord of Misrule back into line. Trump's pre-election pledges to end the wars, rebuild the country's infrastructure with the help of the private sector, and reindustrialize America to make it great again, while simultaneously 'draining the swamp', are floating down the sewers of DC. Bankers are being feted again at the White House while taxes that favour the rich and very rich are enhanced. But what's new? Every president from Reagan to Trump has increased the divide between the mega-rich and the less well-off. Obama's eight years saw the largest gap between the top and lower layers.

The foreign policy front is no different. The decision to order a quick bombing raid on Syria, à la Clinton, and despatch more troops to Afghanistan just like Obama have reassured the extreme centre and its organ, the *New York Times*.[1] Normality is returning to the White House: drones and bombs kill and maim; rude tweets simply entertain. Anti-NATO/EU rhetoric has been toned down, and the British and French are in open competition to see who can get closest to the giant posterior in the White House. The Germans remain grumpy, but are well aware that a breach with Atlanticism is unthinkable at this time.

What of the 2016 election itself? Did it justify the wave of moral hysteria that accompanied it? Or the outpouring of liberal grief, the announcement of a resistance movement, an often-expressed fear that the United States was heading in a fascist direction – that Trump was a fascist, even – that the US political formation was undergoing an irreversible shift?

Mike Davis, one of the country's most gifted social

---

1 During a TV interview with Fox, the new POTUS astonished his interlocutor, who was denouncing Putin as a brutal enforcer, etc. Trump remarked that the US had done some pretty bad things too. This caused shock and horror in the liberal media led by the *NYT*, which fosters the illusion that bad things are necessary to maintain freedom and democracy.

historians, called for calm in the pages of *New Left Review*. He argued,

> We should resist the temptation to over-interpret Trump's election victory. Progressives who think they've woken up in another country should calm down, take a stiff draught and reflect on the actual results from the swing states. First, with the exceptions of Iowa and Ohio, there were no Trump landslides in key states. He merely did as well as Mitt Romney had in 2012, compensating for smaller votes in the suburbs with larger votes in rural areas to achieve the same overall result. His combined margin of victory in Wisconsin, Michigan and Pennsylvania was razor thin, under 78,000 votes. The surprise of the election was not a huge white working-stiff shift to Trump but rather his success in retaining the loyalty of Romney voters, and indeed even slightly improving on the latter's performance amongst evangelicals. Thus, economic populism and nativism potently combined with, but did not displace, the traditional social conservative agenda.

Obama had won all three marginal states twice, thus disproving the suggestion that it was all due to racism. In fact, it was the selection of a much-disliked Democrat candidate, Hillary Rodham Clinton, from a venal political family, coupled with Obama's own failures, that allowed Trump to win. In contrast, Bernie Sanders's campaign revealed a growing radicalism among important sections of the electorate – those who don't normally vote – and a Biden/Sanders or a Warren/Sanders ticket might well have kept Trump out.

It was Clinton and Obama, solidly backed by the liberal media networks, who enforced her candidacy and orchestrated her defeat. Young women preferred Sanders to Clinton, and desperate elderly feminists could not reverse the trend. Furthermore, the candidate was handed a weak legacy. Obama's weaknesses gave the Republicans a majority in House and Senate and fuelled support for Sanders. David Bromwich, writing in the *London Review of Books*, expressed this well:

> The Sanders candidacy emerged in part from fatigue and depression at the long day's end of the Obama presidency. When he began his run, we hardly realised how discouraged we were; and his appeal is warmest and widest with young voters. A large reason for this is his realistic emphasis on the coming catastrophe of planetary climate disruption, an issue on which, thanks to his courage and tenacity, he stands alone among living American politicians. But in other ways too, Sanders represents something fresh, something younger at heart than either Obama or Hillary Clinton. When you come to think of it, he is as unlike Obama as it is possible for a man of the left to be: passionate, but without any theatrical dimension in his show of passion; angry at economic injustice, but with an anger that rises above the intimation of suppressed parental rage. The official statement by Obama in April 2009 that no American citizen would be punished for practising torture, and

the unofficial statement by his attorney general that the leaders of the 'too-big-to-fail' money firms were too important to be punished, rankled with many citizens who believe in one law for rich and poor alike and would like to believe that justice goes all the way into the long driveways of the power elite. Sanders has said that 'too big to fail is too big to exist', and he believes that wickedness in high places ought to be punished.

Despite the grotesqueries on display, despite White House encouragement for the legatees of the Ku Klux Klan and the Third Reich, despite the decline in personal ratings, despite the abandonment of what had been promised, the umbilical cord that ties Trump to his social-conservative base has not yet been broken. Six months after his inauguration, in June 2017, a mini-referendum was on offer. Five seats had fallen vacant in the House: Georgia, Montana, Kansas, California and South Carolina. Four of them fell to the Republicans. The framework of the extreme centre does not encourage an opposition.

Hence the absurd attempt by liberals to demonize Putin in the hope that something might emerge to impeach Trump. It's as if the Clinton–Obama Democrats have given up on politics. They still do not want to accept the fact that their candidate lost because of her own frailties. In the liberal media bubble (see 'A Bouquet o'Schlock' below) Obama could do no wrong, but in the real world he was a disappointment to many of his own once-enthusiastic supporters. His personal ratings remained high but did not translate into political support for the Democrats.

The measures set in place by Bush and the Fed after the 2008 crash were kept in place. The Wall Street sharks avoided punishment altogether, much to their own amazement. The 1 per cent grew richer while inequality deepened. Obamacare did improve the situation by increasing the number of Americans with health insurance by 20 million, but 28 million remain without coverage, and the labyrinthine bureaucratic processes and jargon annoyed even those who benefited. As a result, most Democrat candidates did not mention Obamacare during the campaign.

It is perhaps too early to assess its impact, but the health reforms still needed to reverse life expectancy trends in the United States require a president prepared to take on Big Pharma and the insurance giants. The figures below indicate the two-tier structure of the United States that usually comes to the fore during catastrophes such as New Orleans. The country with the highest per capita GDP in the world is ranked at thiry-nine in life expectancy.

Race and Empire

Trump deliberately unsettled liberal America and sectors of the traditional establishment in order to win the presidency. That he has done so in brutal fashion is a reflection

Life Expectancy and Per Capita GDP at Current Exchange Rates in 2015

Country	Per Capita GDP ($)	Actual Life Expectancy (Years)	Predicted Life Expectancy (Years)	Actual Life Expectancy Compared to Predicted	World Rank in Per Capita GDP	World Rank in Life Expectancy	Rank in Life Expectancy Compared to Rank in Per Capita GDP
Japan	34,474	83.6	80.4	3.2	27	2	25
Italy	30,049	83.1	79.7	3.4	29	5	24
France	36,527	82.7	80.7	2.0	23	7	16
Canada	43,316	82.0	81.5	0.5	16	15	1
UK	43,930	81.3	81.6	−0.3	14	23	−9
Germany	41,177	81.1	81.2	−0.2	19	27	−8
US	56,207	78.7	82.8	−4.0	8	39	−31

Source: Calculated from World Bank World Development Indicators of his particularisms: vain, crude, brattish, a billionaire TV celebrity, misogynist to his very core, equating white supremacy with its victims, and so on. The list is long. But abstracting his personality from what he is actually doing, it's difficult to argue that he is more right-wing than Ronald Reagan, the president eulogized by the Bushes, the Clintons and Obama. Is Trump worse than Nixon? The racism and anti-Semitism revealed in the Watergate tapes shocked many liberals at the time. The main difference with Reagan and Nixon is that Trump says in public what they and many others in the Senate and the House thought in private or said to each other in segregated spaces.

Racism in the United States is *sui generis*, embedded in the origins of the colonial white settlements established by the British Empire that rested ultimately on the genocidal extermination of the country's indigenous population and huge land grabs, early examples of privatisation at the expense of common landholdings. Then came slavery and the transformation of black men and women into beasts of burden, transported in vessels that became breeding grounds for disease and death. The fittest survived and were duly auctioned in the marketplaces of England and its New World colony.

The founding fathers of this bloodstained republic were all white supremacists, a fact clearly reflected in the US constitution. The relatively few Native Americans who survived decades of slaughter and disease were not even allowed to be citizens and confined to their settlements, dependent on handouts from an exterminist post-colonial state. The tragedy of Native Americans was enhanced by the civil war between the Union and the Confederacy that erupted in the middle of the nineteenth century. A number of tribes fought with the Confederacy, reasoning that 'the enemy of my enemy is my friend'. Some changed sides. Some were divided and fought each other. Had the tribes remained aloof from the conflict it might have created a basis for unity against the forked tongues, but this was not to be. After the Civil War the unified state turned on the natives with a vengeance. The demonization and vilification of 'the enemy' during the 'Indian Wars' were faithfully mirrored by Hollywood throughout the twentieth century.

The US Civil War ended slavery as an institution but cemented white supremacy. What essentially began as a constitutional struggle fought by other means soon expanded to encompass the question of slavery. Initially Lincoln pledged that if the secessionist states remained in or rejoined the Union they could maintain slavery. The principal argument used against slavery was that it was inefficient and that freed labour would produce a more satisfactory rate of exploitation and increase profits. The plantation owners remained unconvinced. As the war progressed and Lincoln issued the Emancipation Proclamation, black regiments were created under white command and fought well for the Union. The war ended with Dixie burnt down. Horror stories of Sherman's assault on Atlanta, many of them true, were passed down from generation to generation.

Two separate mythologies arose from the war. The first, and most absurd, was fictionalized as *Gone with the Wind*, later a huge success on celluloid and much more effective – though not as aesthetically interesting – than D. W. Griffith's *Birth of a Nation* (1915), much admired later by Fascist filmmakers and documentarists in Nazi Germany. The second mythology was related to racism in the North. The American ideology that black people were free in the North is true only to the extent that slavery did not exist legally in Northern states, but the conditions in which blacks lived and worked was a form of institutionalized racism that has not disappeared. Slavery was replaced by segregation. This was the basis of the new settlement. The cycle of black politics could be summed up as nightmare, struggle, despair, struggle more, and dream. The lineages of Black Lives Matter stretch back three centuries.

Attempts by the Radical Republicans before, during and after the Civil War to ensure that the state granted equal rights to all its citizens resulted in the Reconstruction, which for a period divided the South into military zones presided over by Union generals. The Radical Republicans pressed Lincoln to dismantle the white power structure below the Mason–Dixon line. Before the war had been conclusively decided, two prominent leaders,

Benjamin Wade and Henry Winter Davis, sponsored a bill proposing rule by provisional governors in the South till the time when a majority of the white male population swore loyalty to the Union. The bill was passed in 1864, but Lincoln refused to sign it. White reconciliation was his principal priority, and for that reason he had selected as his vice president a deeply reactionary, but effective, leader of the poor whites in the South, Andrew Johnson.[2]

In 1865 Johnson, now president following the assassination of Lincoln, vetoed Radical Republican attempts to strengthen the Freedmen's Bureau, established by Congress after the war. The Bureau had been created to improve living conditions for former slaves. The sum of $17 million had been allocated by the Union to

---

2 November 1867: The Judiciary Committee votes 5–4 to impeach Johnson for 'high crimes and misdemeanours'. These include presidential pardons for Civil War traitors, corruption (profiting from the illegal disposal of railroads in Tennessee), defying Congress, blocking all attempts to reconstruct the South and the ratification of the 14th Amendment; 30 March 1868: Johnson's impeachment trial begins. He is the only president of the United States to suffer such a fate, though many others have deserved it. The trial, held in the Senate, was presided over by Chief Justice Salmon Chase. The Radical Republicans almost won. The result was 35 to 19, one vote short of the required two-thirds majority for conviction. It was alleged that two mainstream Republicans had been bought off, which has a ring of truth.

create 4,000 new schools, 100 new hospitals and publicly funded housing for freed families. In April 1866, Johnson vetoed the Civil Rights Act, passed by Congress, the aim of which was to protect freed slaves from the notorious 'black codes' that made a mockery of what they had won. Freed slaves were not allowed to vote, to sit on juries, to give testimony against whites, or to carry weapons in public. A number of occupations were sealed off, restricting their employment rights.

Angry Republicans decided to impeach Johnson, and Charles Sumner, one of the leaders of the Radical Republicans, said of the fight against his president,

> This is one of the last great battles with slavery. Driven from the legislative chambers, driven from the field of war, this monstrous power has found a refuge in the executive mansion, where, in utter disregard of the Constitution and laws, it seeks to exercise its ancient, far-reaching sway. All this is very plain. Nobody can question it. Andrew Johnson is the impersonation of the tyrannical slave power. In him it lives again. He is the lineal successor of John C. Calhoun and Jefferson Davis; and he gathers about him the same supporters.

Encouraged by the president's show of support, former Confederate generals, officers and soldiers set up the first branch of the Ku Klux Klan in Tennessee, targeting African Americans, European immigrants and Radical Republican supporters. Its first Grand Wizard was Nathan

Bedford Forrest, a Confederate general, who remains to this day a celebrated figure in the South.[3]

From 1868–70, the Klan helped to restore white supremacy in North Carolina, Tennessee and Georgia. Smaller supremacist sects – the White Brotherhood, Constitutional Union Guards, Knights of the White Camelia – all of them armed, were assigned the virtually full-time task of physically preventing black people from registering to vote or visiting polling places. That was their day job. After supper, they burnt down black businesses. White supremacy was considered more sacred than the right to private property. The Civil War was a huge victory for preserving the Union and restricting North America to only two states. It was a pyrrhic victory for the slaves. Michelle Alexander has demonstrated how today the number of African Americans incarcerated or working their way through the judicial system exceeds the number who were enslaved on the eve of the civil war.[4]

It would take a century before desegregation was imposed on Southern cities. It was never fully accepted,

---

3　Forrest's statue was under attack in August 2017 by black and white protesters. In general I am not in favour of destroying statues that mark a historical period. It would be much better to insist upon an alternative biography or narrative to stimulate debate. But there are definitely exceptions and Forrest is one of them ... even the automatic playing of Billy Holliday singing 'Strange Fruit' every fifteen minutes should not be enough to save this statue.

4　Michelle Alexander, *The New Jim Crow* (New York, 2012) p. 180.

and white supremacist groups, albeit in greatly reduced numbers, flanked by armed vigilantes have since maintained a subterranean presence (for a long time their public face in many cities, South and North, was the police force). How can they be anything but grateful to a president who offers them a public platform?

The brutal assertion of white supremacy in Emancipation Park, Charlottesville, in August 2017 and Trump's equivocations on the matter sent a sharp message to his opponents. Have no doubt, he signalled, this president belongs to an old supremacist tradition that fuelled the mainstream political parties till the 1960s. Some commentators have argued that the only reason he behaves in this fashion is to keep his supporters on side. I don't buy this. Racial prejudice is embedded in Trump's psyche. What else explains the bizarre decision to override the courts and offer a presidential pardon to Joe Arpaio, a former Arizona sheriff convicted of racial profiling? There were many other ways of maintaining support among his base: reindustrialization, the regulation of Wall Street, repairing national infrastructure, job creation. All this was promised during the campaign.

Right-wing politics in the United States is nothing new, despite the victories of liberal Democrats from time to time. Even during the sixties, when mainly white college students and adult African Americans galvanized the country with the help of GIs returning from Vietnam, there was always the other side. The images were of students being gassed and jailed in their hundreds, of black militants being slaughtered and bombed. Malcolm X, Martin Luther King, Fred Hampton, and George Jackson paid with their lives, and being too liberal led to the assassination of the Kennedy brothers.

The killings at Jackson State and Kent State universities were part of the process of weeding out the enemies at home. And the alt-right of the time greeted the repression with hosannas. In the case of Kent State, where four students were shot dead by National Guard troops, a horror story emerged. Three brothers from near the Kentucky border studied on the campus. Two of them were caught up in the student strike against the war, but had no prior record of protest. They were not on any list but were photographed. Meanwhile the younger brother had been one of the hundreds arrested for trespass. A year later researchers interviewed their mother. She was not a member of any party, leave alone a far-right group. In other words, a fairly ordinary, hard-working woman, shaken by events. The researchers were startled by her responses:

> MOTHER: Anyone who appears on the streets of a city like Kent with long hair, dirty clothes or barefooted deserves to be shot.
> RESEARCHER: Have I your permission to quote that?
> M: You sure do. It would have been better if the [National] Guard had shot the whole lot of them that morning.
> R: But you had three sons there.

213

M: If they didn't do what the Guards told them, they should have been mowed down.

PROFESSOR OF PSYCHOLOGY (listening in): Is long hair justification for shooting someone?

M: Yes. We have got to clean up this nation. And we'll start with the long-hairs.

P: Would you permit one of your sons to be shot simply because he went barefooted?

M: Yes.

P: Where do you get such ideas?

M: I teach at the local high school.

P: You mean you are teaching your students such things?

M: Yes, I teach them the truth. That the lazy, the dirty, the ones you see walking the streets and doing nothing ought all to be shot.[5]

These views, minus the vigour, were not uncommon in the United States. They reflected the 'common sense' of many families. Underlying such ideas was the fact that as citizens of an imperial state their well-being was related to the success of the nation. The anti-war movement and the high rate of US casualties in Vietnam jolted many people, but a sizeable section remained solid, backing Reagan and Bush to the hilt and transferring this loyalty to Bill Clinton and Obama when they exercised imperial power. Trump, despite campaign promises to the contrary, is

---

5   James A. Michener, *Kent State: What Happened and Why?* (New York, 1971), pp. 409ff.

carrying on with the wars. He authorized more troops for Afghanistan, threatens to erase North Korea from the map, supports Saudi atrocities in the Yemen, etc. Nothing has changed on this front.

The US and Spanish empires share this one important attribute in common. The Spaniards had fought against their own people (Spanish Muslims) and were ideologically and militarily prepared for the conquest of South America. The United States likewise: exterminism, as far as Native Americans were concerned, and white supremacy against the slaves and black freed men and women had prepared the Union army to expand its frontiers westwards. The defence of capitalism required counter-revolutions at home and, later, abroad. The destruction of every habitable building in North Korea in the early fifties was followed by rape, torture of the vilest sort, and a total disregard for civilian live in Vietnam throughout the sixties.

Trump's promises to stop foreign interventions were never credible. Confronted economically by the rise of China, the US Empire is more determined than before to maintain its military stranglehold on every continent. There are few signs of decline in the ideological and military realms. Even the economic decline is greatly overplayed and often confused with the sad state of the social infrastructure and the decline of public education.

Where are we going to end up at the end of this century? What role will China play? Is Western democracy going to flourish? One thing that has become clear over the last decades is that nothing happens unless people want it to happen; and if people want it to happen, they start moving.

Desperate problems confront the military–political leaders of the United States every single day in some part of the globe. Exercising imperial power is different from playing golf. Trump may be back under control, but the energy spent by the State Department and the Pentagon in keeping him contained is distracting. And they're already beginning to ask each other whether he might win another term. In public there is talk of impeachment; in private there are whispers of another solution.

The midterms in autumn 2018 will offer some clues, but it is the lack of an effective opposition that is hollowing out American democracy. The Democrats have long been part of the problem. Desperately needed social and structural reforms were ignored by Bill Clinton and Obama. The first wallowed in his popularity, especially among African Americans ('Our first black president' in Toni Morrison's memorable words); the second enjoyed being treated as a Hollywood celebrity. Both these men and Hillary mingled lovingly with billionaire donors, hoping that some of the wealth might rub off. It did. The political insurgency unleashed by Sanders laid siege to the Clinton–Obama fortress but could not break down the barriers. It is doubtful whether they will next time. Jesse Jackson's Rainbow Coalition had tried and failed on a previous occasion. That defeat had seen off Jackson. The black caucus of Democrats in Congress is, in the main, a collection of opportunists, little different in outlook from most of their white colleagues.

A third party is badly needed, one capable of uniting the grassroots that fuelled the Sanders campaign, a new generation of activists that was seriously attempting something new. A coalition with a radical but realistic programme and concentrating on winning representatives in specially targeted cities and states, while maintaining a national presence via campaigns and demonstrations, including those that demand the dismantling of US bases abroad as well as an end to the accompanying wars. This is a litmus test that most liberals fail. Like the Fabians of the British Empire, the left liberals who write in the literary and political weeklies mostly accept the benign nature of some, if not all, US interventions. Mark Twain and other writers and philosophers who set up the Anti-Imperialist League over a century ago had a much better idea of their country's destructive capacities. Their equivalents of today loved being feted at the White House by Clinton and Obama. They opposed Bush's war on Iraq, but were less visible during Clinton's murderous sanctions that led to tens of thousands of Iraqi deaths. Had Obama invaded Iraq, the liberal opposition to the war would have been muted. Liberal cosmopolitanism is little else but a moth-infested cover for US imperialist interests.

Success in any new political endeavour, if it is not to disappear after a short burst of struggle, will not be immediate, but the political space exists. It needs to be occupied.

A BOUQUET O' SCHLOCK

A leader of rare talents, anointed with his nation's dreams.
— *Economist*, 22 December 2016:

He has a tragic realist's understanding of sin, cowardice, and corruption, and a Hobbesian appreciation of how fear shapes human behaviour ... who will hand to his successor a set of tools an accomplished assassin would envy ... And yet he consistently, and with apparent sincerity, professes optimism that the world is bending toward justice ... 'I am very much the internationalist', Obama said in a later conversation. 'And I am also an idealist insofar as I believe that we should be promoting values, like democracy and human rights and norms and values, because not only do they serve our interests the more people adopt values that we share – in the same way that, economically, if people adopt rule of law and property rights and so forth, that is to our advantage – but because it makes the world a better place.

— Jeffrey Goldberg, ex-prison guard of the Israeli Defence
Force, in his 17,000-word, multiple colour-photo hymn to
the president, 'The Obama Doctrine. How He's Shaped
the World', *Atlantic*, August 2016, 'informed by our recent
series of conversations, which took place in the Oval Office;
over lunch in his dining room; aboard Air Force One; and
in Kuala Lumpur during his most recent visit to Asia'.

On the way out of the pavilion, Obama signed a few books, posed for some pictures, and seemed distinctly pleased with the way things were going. 'I'm like Mick Jagger,' he said. 'I'm old, I'm gray, but people still turn out.' In the car, riding back to the Charlotte airport, Obama slumped in his seat and read a few e-mails on his phone. Then he brought up a video of the White House Halloween party ... He never loses his capacity to be the scholar of his own predicament, a gently quizzical ethnographer of his own country, of its best and worst qualities ... Here was the hopeful vision of diversity and dignity that Obama had made his own.

> – David Remnick, ex-chronicler of Russia's
> days of freedom under Yeltsin and Gaidar,
> *New Yorker*, 28 November 2016

Rolling Stone has had a wonderful relationship with Obama over the years. I first met him at the beginning of his 2008 campaign, when he came up to my office for dinner. We backed him when he was up and when he was down. He viewed *Rolling Stone* readers as part of his base. A year ago, we went to Alaska with him and toured the melting glaciers. With extraordinary pride, we watched him ride the wave of history ... I had hoped to look back on what he had achieved over eight years and the issues that mattered the most to him and to the readers of *Rolling Stone*, hear his advice for Hillary and about the road ahead. It was to be the 'exit interview', his tenth cover for *Rolling Stone*, our fourth interview together.

– Jan Wenner, *Rolling Stone*, 26 November 2016

On this crisp October night, everything felt inevitable and grand. There was a slight wind. It had been in the 80s for much of that week. Now, as the sun set, the season remembered its name. Women shivered in their cocktail dresses. Gentlemen chivalrously handed over their suit coats. But when Naomi Campbell strolled past the security pen in a sleeveless number, she seemed as invulnerable as ever.

Cell phones were confiscated to prevent surreptitious recordings from leaking out ... The Obamas are social with Beyoncé and Jay-Z. They hosted Chance the Rapper and Frank Ocean at a state dinner, and last year invited Swizz Beatz, Busta Rhymes, and Ludacris, among others, to discuss criminal-justice reform and other initiatives.

– Ta-Nehisi Coates, the new James Baldwin,
Atlantic, January–February 2017

There is a clear, shining line connecting Lincoln and King, and President Obama ... It's a vision of America as an unfinished project – a continuing, more-than-two-century journey to make the promises of the Declaration of Independence real for everyone – rooted both in Scripture and the possibility of redemption, and a more existential belief that we can continually remake ourselves ... He had lunch last week with five novelists he admires – Dave Eggers, Mr Whitehead, Zadie Smith, Mr Diaz and Barbara Kingsolver. He not only talked with them about the political and media landscape, but also talked shop, asking how their book tours were going and remarking that he liked to write first drafts, long hand, on yellow legal pads.

– Michiko Kakutani, literary arbiter of the newspaper of record *New York Times*, 16 January 2017

(Collected by Perry Anderson, 'Passing the Baton',
New Left Review 103, January–February 2017)

8

What's Left in France?

'Today', declared Louis-Napoléon Bonaparte in 1844 (as demands for democracy were growing and the 1848 upheaval was only four years away), 'the reign of castes is over; one can govern only with the masses.' Emmanuel Macron, the latest Fifth Republic president to fantasize about being a combination of Jupiter, Napoleon and Louis XIV, is, in reality, a tawdry version of the Emperor's nephew. With democracy becoming increasingly ritualized and hollowed out, in France as much as elsewhere, he could easily declare, 'Today the reign of castes is over; one can only govern against the masses.'

The new prime minister, Édouard Philippe, makes little secret of this fact. In an interview with the *Financial Times* the former protégé of French conservative leader Alain

Juppé explained patiently that Macron's government was following the policies of the centre-right. When it was pointed out that his policies – 'flexible' labour markets, tax cuts for the rich, and an assault on public expenditure – were firmly right-wing measures, Mr Philippe chortled: 'Yes, what did you expect?'[1]

The April 2017 French general election result was, in some ways, the most explosive in Europe. With the two traditional 'extreme centre' parties wrecked, and the majority of the electorate fearful and desperate at the thought of an extreme-right victory, many flocked to the banner of a Bonapartist banker whose new party was a de facto merger of the worst elements of the French extreme centre. This is a National Government that wishes to dismantle what's left of the French 'exception' and turn it into a half-Atlantic, half-German hybrid.

One of the principal reasons for the victory of Macron was that the only candidate standing against him was Marine Le Pen. She is, of course, from the extreme right, but a sense of panic gripped the establishment. There was a possibility that Jean-Luc Mélenchon, the leader of La France Insoumise (Defiant France), might be able to defeat Le Pen and challenge Macron, but here the French elite was less worried. Nonetheless, the media apparatuses of the extreme centre – petty, spiteful, malicious,

1   Anne-Sylvaine Chassany and Michael Stothard, 'Macron Agenda Puts Right-Leaning PM at Ease', *Financial Times*, 11 July 2017.

unashamedly indulging in the most brazen distortions —
were well prepared.

In their determination to ensure Macron fought Marine
Le Pen in the second round, the tame satirical weekly *Le
Canard Enchaîné*, was fed with information to discredit
the conservative leader, François Fillon, who was accused
of bending rules to put his Welsh wife on the payroll.
Exit Fillon in the first round. Calumnies and defama-
tions were hurled non-stop at Mélenchon. This made
any serious discussion of Defiant France's real shortcom-
ings and defects virtually impossible. Furthermore, if the
media onslaught failed, the extreme-centrists could rely
on the holier-than-thou groupuscules of the far left, long
past their sell-by date, to field their own candidates, each
'purer' than the other and all combining to ensure that
the impure Mélenchon could not challenge Macron. Thus
was lost the only opportunity that would have made the
political debate in France meaningful.

The Socialist Party (PS) was out of the race from
the start. After five years in the Élysée Palace, François
Hollande's ratings were down to 4 per cent and his party
was virtually obliterated at the ballot box. Hollande, a
witty raconteur at private dinner parties, had proved
himself utterly useless at the Élysée. He antagonised
both wings of his own party. He pledged that he would
punish finance capital for its excesses, and to renegoti-
ate the euro. This pleased the left. He promised the right
that he would push through a whole set of regressions

(usually described as 'reforms') to boost capitalism and bring it more into line with the Anglo-American system. The combination would help solve the huge problem of unemployment in France. In the end all sides felt let down and he was abandoned by the electorate. The war in Mali, the strongman image cultivated after the terrorist attacks in France, legalising gay marriage (the only real division with the right and the Church) had all come to nought.

The French elite and its institutions should not have been that hostile. After all, he gave them a lot. He reduced employers' taxes, he deregulated labour laws, and he cut some social welfare benefits as well. The total gain for the bourgeoisie amounted to €70 billion. One could be forgiven for thinking that the final figure was impressive. Too little, too late is what the ungrateful beneficiaries said to each other.

Macron had been François Hollande's private secretary for two years and his finance minister for slightly longer. Hollande once boasted: 'Macron, *cest moi*.' But, having observed this history of political failure from close quarters, Macron kept his distance from the Hollande–Valls team knowing that failure can be infectious. Nevertheless, with Le Pen as his opponent, he knew he could never lose.

Macron decided he could afford to be relatively frank regarding his real aims. He could also raise AHB (Art of the Higher Bullshit) levels way beyond the standard. His campaign was therefore studded with examples such as the following half-baked reflections, drawn from Macron's obligatory election-year book, *Révolution*:

> I am very Camusian ... I learnt from Colette what was a flower, from Giono a cold wind in Provence and the truth of characters. Gide and Cocteau were my irreplaceable companions ... I took the road of characters in Flaubert, Hugo. I was consumed by the ambition of Balzac's young bloods ... André Breton, who loved Paris so well, arrived one day by chance in the backland of the Lot and cried: *I have stopped wanting to be anywhere else.* I will never tire of contemplating the motionless, fugitive soul of France.[2]

And much else besides. Sartre was spared a mention, though what is really needed to deal with Macron's France is the inimitable poison pen of Louis-Ferdinand Céline. He would have understood.

Macron's victory was, however, a huge success for French capital. In contrast to Hollande's failures, Sarkozy's vanity and greed, Fillon's arrogance, Macron was carefully constructed as a new makeover candidate. It has worked, but how long can the effect last? A columnist in the *Financial Times*, a newspaper that Macron regularly reads, compared him to an actor named Tony Blair:

---

2 Quoted in Perry Anderson's bracing editorial 'The French Spring' in *New Left Review* 105, May–June 2017.

> Like Blair, Macron enjoys meeting people who are angry
> with him, because he trusts his charm to win them over ...
> To imagine how this might end, remember Blair. His faith
> in his own star convinced him he was right about Iraq's
> supposed weapons of mass destruction. He then charmed par-
> liament and voters into war. Nobody forgives being seduced
> and then deceived, which is why most Britons now despise
> Blair.

The French presidential election was the exact opposite of the general election in Britain. Whereas the latter restored the standing of the two traditional parties, with Labour's manifesto marking a clear break with the extreme centre, in France the two major parties of the centre were destroyed by a remarkable campaign waged by the French banking elite. This propelled a clever centre-extremist, Emmanuel Macron, and his hurriedly created political outfit to power.

And yet there was something about Macron that was unconvincing to many French citizens. His actual vote was lower than predicted. Abstentions on the second round of the presidential election reached 24.44 per cent (12.1 million votes), and there was a record number of blank or spoiled votes (4.07 million). The honeymoon did not last too long either. Within weeks of the formation of a new government, two cabinet ministers, an ex-Socialist and a right-wing centrist, had to resign when their misuse of public money was exposed. Not long afterwards the

French military chief of staff criticised the defence cuts being proposed and resigned. Only a few days prior to this clash, Macron and visiting imperial leader Donald Trump were cavorting with the military and Macron was putting on his toughest look.

Even the most dedicated militants of the informal league of sycophants who surround every new president began to look slightly nervous. Their fears were justified. An opinion poll revealed that Macron's much-vaunted ratings had plummeted by ten percentage points, a higher rate of decline than that of Sarkozy and Hollande at the same stage. The kiss of death might well be Bono's quick visit for a photo-op with the first lady.

Failure was further compounded in Macron's copycat US-exec-style 'state of the union message' to the combined houses of parliament at the Palace of Versailles. Neatly combining 'past glories' and history (the Versaillais against the Communards) with presentist fantasies, Macron declared that the 'new start' he symbolised had brought back 'optimism and hope' to France. The speech was as market-driven and market-oriented as everything else he proposed. He promised to bring the West Coast to Versailles, and since there was no longer an Atlantic, France could easily become 'a nation of start-ups' and 'attract foreign talents'. In his speeches on the need for migrants, Macron has discarded the racism of the Socialist former prime minister Manuel Valls, while emphasizing that what he means by encouraging immigrants is an appeal to graduates and postgraduates. Silicon Valley, his message seemed to say, please move to Le Touquet.[3]

Macron's stunning triumph has energised the politicians of the extreme centre. The achievement of Defiant France and its leader, Jean-Luc Mélenchon, pales by comparison, but it would be foolish to underestimate it. The 19.58 per cent obtained in the first round of the presidential vote was the highest for a candidate to the left of the SP since 1969, a very different political time. Apart from defending the welfare state and propounding an anti-war foreign policy, Defiant France campaigned for a Sixth Republic, a new form of parliamentary democracy. Mélenchon argued for a new constitution. In 1958, after the coup that imposed the Fifth Republic, General de Gaulle had ranted against the 'party system'. In 2017, Macron has deployed his demagogy against the 'political class' to which he belongs. In 1958 France was confronting the consequences of its brutal war in Algeria. Today the crisis is economic, the result of a long downturn exacerbated by the Wall Street crash of 2008. Deindustrialization has pushed millions of workers out of their jobs. In July 2017, there were 5.9 million unemployed workers.

French politicians of the extreme centre, backed by a decaying intelligentsia and a sycophantic mediocracy,

---

3   Like Birnham Wood to Dunsinane as the witches warned Macbeth? A majority in France according to the latest polls are opposed to any new labour law introduced by presidential decree, as Macron wants. The Californication of France is some way off yet.

sought a solution whose roots stretched back to the thirties. They targeted the country's Muslim minority (approximately 4.7 million out of a total of 66.8 million citizens). What was once the preserve of the Le Pen family was now a prejudice invoked by Sarkozy and strongly adopted by Prime Minster Manuel Valls. Rather than focusing on the ills of 'the economy, stupid', the politicians saw the major threat coming from 'a larger project of civilization, identity and culture'. Thus as anti-Semitism, real and imagined, was severely reprimanded and punished, Islamophopia became the norm. To his credit, Macron refused to climb on this bandwagon, treating the 'debate on identity' as irrelevant and visiting Algiers at the height of the campaign to denounce French colonialism as 'a crime against humanity'. He did not visit Mali or Libya. But with a new terrorist attack, Macron could easily shift.

Such scenes were witnessed in January 2015. In the week following the *Charlie Hebdo* atrocities, a wave of moral hysteria swept France. 'Je suis Charlie' became almost obligatory. The Hollande–Valls message was simple: either you were for the magazine or for the terrorists. Quite a few, now as in 2001, were for neither. These included Henri Roussel, the eighty-year-old co-founding editor of *Hara-Kiri*, the magazine's first incarnation, banned by the French government for insulting the corpse of Charles de Gaulle. In a remarkable essay published in the *Nouvel Observateur*, Roussel made two essential points that were not made by any politician, including Macron. The first concerned French foreign policy:

> I don't much like it when a head of state speaks of the dead as heroes. It usually happens because citizens have been sent to war and not come back, which is rather the case with the victims of the attack on *Charlie Hebdo*. The attack is part of a war declared on France, but can also be seen in the light of the wars France has got itself involved in: conflicts where its participation isn't called for, where worse massacres than that at *Charlie Hebdo* take place every day, several times a day, where our bombardments pile death on death in the hope of saving potentates who feel threatened and are no better than those who threaten them … If Obama had not held Hollande back, he would have gone after Assad in Syria, just as Sarkozy went after Gaddafi in Libya … with the result we're familiar with.

The second was personal. Roussel knew all the victims well and this made him both angry and sorrowful. He denounced Stéphane 'Charb' Charbonnier, the magazine's late editor, for his recklessness:

> He was the boss. Why did he need to drag the whole team into it? In the first attack on *Charlie Hebdo* in November 2011, the offices were torched after an issue was called 'Charia Hebdo'. I quote what I said … in the *Obs*: 'I think we're ignorant and imbeciles who have taken a pointless risk. That's all. We think

we're invulnerable. For years, decades even, we do provocative things and then one day the provocation comes back at us. It didn't need to be done.'

It didn't need to be done, but Charb did it again. A year later, in September 2012, after a provocation that put France's ambassadors in Muslim countries in a state of siege ... I asked Charb in the pages of the *Obs*: 'To show, with the caption "Muhammed: A Star is Born", a naked Muhammed praying, seen from behind, balls dangling and prick dripping, in black and white but with a yellow star on his anus – whatever way you look at it, how is this funny?'

I was sick of it. Charb told a journalist from *Le Monde*: 'I have no kids, no wife, I prefer to die on my feet than to live on my knees.' Cavanna, who feared death, wrote when he was Charb's age: 'Rather red than dead.'[4] The reds are no longer red, the dead are still dead. Everyone has seen Charb's last cartoon: 'Still no attacks in France?' And the jihadist in the cartoon, armed like the one who killed Charb, Tignous, Cabu, Honoré and the others, replies: 'Wait! We've got until the end of January for New Year's greetings ...' Have you seen Wolinski's last cartoon? It ends: 'I dream of returning to Cuba to drink rum, smoke a cigar and dance with the beautiful Cuban girls.'

Charb who preferred to die and Wolin who preferred to live. I blame you, Charb. Peace on your soul.

---

4   François Cavanna (1923–2014) worked with Rousel on *Hara-Kiri* and *Charlie Hebdo*.

Roussel's was a lonely voice and, in response to complaints, including one from the publisher of *Charlie Hebdo*, the editor of *Nouvel Observateur* replied that after serious discussion it had been agreed that freedom of speech was best preserved by not denying it to those who disagreed with the mainstream narrative. Elsewhere three publishers who refused to display 'Je suis Charlie' on their websites were subjected to persistent questioning and bullying.

And what of the huge Sunday crowd convened by the president at the Place de la République? The photo-op brigade in the vanguard met with disaster when Netanyahu, waving triumphantly to onlookers, crashed his way to the front. The dignitaries he was so keen to join weren't all that impressive: the puppet president of Mali; Angela Merkel, the Mother of Europe (her hands held in a way that suggested a mysterious Masonic signal); and Donald Tusk, the Polish president of the Council of Europe. And, hurriedly summoned at the last minute to balance the presence of the Israeli leader, there was Mahmoud Abbas, the PLO leader, holding hands with the king of Jordan. Sarkozy, placed in the fourth row, quickly began his own long march to the front, but by the time he got there the cameras had disappeared and the celebs soon followed suit. How many turned up in all? A million was the official figure. Eric Hazan, the waspish historian of Paris, used different criteria:

It was as big as the one on 28 April 1944, when Marshal Pétain attended the funeral service for the victims of Allied bombings at the Hôtel de Ville. War fever apart (the shouts of 'To Berlin!' in 1914), the great moments of unanimity have taken place at public funerals – like those of Victor Hugo, Pierre Overney, Jean-Paul Sartre, or Edith Piaf. Sunday's demonstration is of the same order, the crowd is moved by sentiment and satisfied by coming together to express a vague desire for unity and reconciliation. As if the strength of the crowd was enough to mitigate the lack of a society that takes our common well-being as its goal.

Slowly, however, a more critical France began to speak up. An opinion poll two days after the big march revealed a divided country: 57 per cent were 'Je suis Charlie's, but 42 per cent were opposed to hurting the feelings of minorities. Some of the latter might have been thinking of the blanket publicity for Michel Houellebecq and his new novel, *Soumission*, on TV and in print in the week preceding the attack on the magazine. Those with longer memories might have recalled Houellebecq's statement in 2001, which laid the basis for the title of his latest offering: 'Reading the Quran is a disgusting experience. Ever since Islam's birth it has been distinguished by its desire to make the world submit to itself. Submission is its very nature.'

With the passing of the old order, as far as political parties are concerned, is France entering a period of relative stability? I don't think so. Underneath, the mood is volatile (there were exceptionally high abstentions in the second round and parliamentary elections); the loyal *macaroon* Isabelle Huppert can often be heard sighing with displeasure at the speed with which many of her friends are abandoning Jupiter, who is already displaying signs that he is running out of breath. Infrastructure is slowly decaying and social polarization continues apace. Harmony does not seem to be on any agenda. The traditional French right has decapitated itself. On the extreme right Marine Le Pen's defeat, hardly a surprise, has opened up fissures inside her own party and there is much talk of a split led by her niece.

On the left the electoral rise of Defiant France is a huge opportunity to construct a political party of a new type, unifying various struggles, thinking strategically and dialectically about both the changes that are needed and those that are possible. Above all, such a party needs to be a strong opposition and on every level, not just coming to life during electoral cycles.

The old far left retreated into its various shells a few years back, repeating timeless truths and, with a few exceptions (which included the late Daniel Bensaïd and Pierre Bourdieu), incapable of confronting the post-Marxist intelligentsia by thinking creatively. With the emergence of the extreme centre, the foundational divide between conservatism and traditional social democracy evaporated. The vacuum boosted the far right, and

Trump's victory in the US frightened many towards the extreme centre. The left, till the rise of Corbyn in Britain and the large vote for Defiant France, was in a bad state in most of Europe and North America. The patches of blue sky need to be expanded. Meanwhile Jupiter's ratings continue to fall. He polls now lower (at 36 per cent) than François Hollande at this stage in his presidency. And it's always useful to remember that a large majority in France did not vote for neoliberal regressions. Macron's first round vote of 24 per cent is the extent of his core support and even this might soon begin to decline.

The following conversation with Olivier Tonneau of France Defiant provides a view from inside the Mélenchon campaign:

TARIQ ALI: The way in which the presidential campaign has been reported in the Euro-American media is as a victory for reason, for rationality and neoliberal capitalism. A general sigh of relief. France didn't let us down. It found the perfect candidate, but a great deal of help was provided. Fillon's exposure was not an accident, suggesting the French state was involved in manipulating the succession to Hollande. How did they manage it so smoothly?

OLIVIER TONNEAU: Well it is hard to tell. I think, of course, I agree with what you just said, and it is very striking that Macron was Hollande's private secretary for two years then a minister of finance for another two, and they managed to rebrand him as the radical new thing, and a radical change in French politics. But his supporters shouldn't get too carried away.

How did they manage to do it? Actually, perhaps, the answer is that they are overrating their success. If you look at opinion polls, they reveal that Macron has a tiny base of support. There was one poll that showed only 8 per cent of the French population supported his programme. So, there is in a sense a very big failure here. And what you said that 'it had been crucial to pick him against Le Pen' is precisely a sign of the fact that they themselves knew that they will not manage to build consensus around these candidates. So, the only solution was to make him run against Le Pen as a sort of *repoussoir*, an untouchable. The real story should be: how did they manage to build up Le Pen? And as a Mélenchon supporter, this is something I have witnessed first-hand for years and which infuriated me.

Let's take one example of a typical strategy. As you know, Le Pen has been stealing many, many elements in our programme in order to appeal to working-class constituencies. Every time Mélenchon was on the news, the question was put to him, 'Your programme is the same as that of Marine Le Pen, how do you explain that?' If they had been factual, journalists would have said, 'Le Pen has stolen your programme,' you just needed to compare the dates, you know, when does one measure appear on the Mélenchon programme and when does it appear on

Le Pen's programme. They would never do this. They would accuse Mélenchon of copying Le Pen.

Now, by equating constantly Le Pen and Mélenchon, what was the effect? On middle classes, the effect was to say, 'Because Mélenchon is like Le Pen, he, too, is an untouchable and therefore cannot win.' You cannot vote for this guy. As for the working-class constituency, the message was, well, since Le Pen is offering [the same as] Mélenchon is offering then why bother vote for Mélenchon; just keep on voting for Le Pen. This is just one example that was constantly engineered to boost Le Pen as the working-class candidate and reduce Mélenchon as an alternative.

Then there are other simple data such as the media exposure of the different candidates. Macron had something like 40 per cent of the total media coverage of all the candidates, and Le Pen also scores very highly – much, much higher than Mélenchon. What can one do?

TA: Two other points need to be made here. First, it is worth remembering that when Marine's father, Jean-Marie Le Pen, stood for the presidency the first time, the positions of the FN on Europe and the economy were virtually indistinguishable from those of Macron today. The Front National were staunch supporters of the EU till Maastricht and of the free market too. So, this shift has been very carefully planned by their leadership and by Marine, in particular, to try and win some class support, which she succeeded in doing.

But the more interesting thing is this: when Jean-Marie Le Pen became the possible choice in a two-horse race in the second round, 80 per cent of France voted Chirac. They said, 'We did it holding our nose.' This time fewer people wanted to hold their noses and vote Macron, which means that there was probably the largest abstention in French electoral history, which is in itself quite astonishing and shows that the elite might not be able to complete this operation.

OT: Absolutely. I think that is correct. The two big differences from 2002. The first difference is the solidification of the Front National vote. There are very good studies that show that up until 2012 the Front National vote remained volatile. People voted once in their life for the Front National as a protest against the mainstream parties. It was during François Hollande's presidency that the FN actually grew strong roots, which shows that perfidy from the left always has much worse consequences than a betrayal from the right. From the right it's not a betrayal, it's a simple application of their programme.

The other side of the equation is that I think in 2002 everybody perceived the qualification of Le Pen for the second round as an accident. You probably remember that the left was divided and that Lionel Jospin, the Socialist candidate, failed to reach the second round by something ridiculous, some tenth of a point. In 2017, there was a strong instinct that we had been set up. That everything had been done to lead us here and, therefore, there was a very strong refusal to give in.

There was a sense of really being humiliated – 'Now we got the scenario we wanted, you just go down and do what we told you to do.' So, for a lot of the people on the left that was impossible. And, also, it is also clear this strategy of always saying, 'Vote for anybody because we have Le Pen in front of you,' that at some point it has to stop. This is also why Mélenchon did not give instructions for a second-round vote. There was a sense that if you give in now, then you're going to give in forever.

TA: I thought this was an important step forward for French left politics, not to do the bidding of the rulers of the country and their ideological apparatuses, which is what they wanted you to do, but to draw back and make an independent analysis.

OT: I'm glad you say that because, as you know, not everybody on the left agrees with your assessment on this. What is really crucial, nonetheless, is that Mélenchon gave one very clear instruction: not one vote for the FN. This is very important because some people spin his position as if he was saying Le Pen and Macron are the same. This is not the case. That would be a total exaggeration.

The other thing worth remembering is that one concrete achievement was that we won back working-class and youth votes from the FN. We have many concrete examples of this, people who did vote FN in the past swinging towards Mélenchon. Also people who had been abstaining for decades suddenly decided to return to politics in order to vote for Mélenchon. And these people only did this because they felt that we were offering a radical break from the system. Getting instructions would have been detrimental to this so it was not an option.

TA: In the past there has been 'cohabitation' with a right-wing president and a Socialist prime minister backed by a majority in the Assembly. But this is rare and the general trend is to give a new president the benefit of the doubt. This is what has happened again with the different coloured *macaroons* on display: bandwagon careerists flocking from both wings of the crumbling extreme centre.

OT: One possibility, of course, would have been to elect us, since the cornerstone of our programme is the convocation of a Constituent Assembly to move to a Sixth Republic. I think that this is very problematic. Normally there should theoretically be at least a balance of power between the executive power and the parliament, which holds the legislative power. But it never works because of the party and electoral system [first-past-the-post as in Britain] created by the Fifth Republic.

TA: Macron seems to be falling fast, but nonetheless his triumph should not be underestimated. The *Economist* had him on its cover as the man on the white horse coming to rescue the EU. For me he is an identikit extreme-centre politician. We are going to be horrible to you but with smiling faces and designer clothes. How do you see him?

OT: I agree. He's a very bizarre synthetic product. A chameleon with a hard neoliberal core. If you look at his body language, it's characteristic of Sarkozy. He moves his shoulders like Sarkozy. If you look at his very crass, liberal credo, [it] is characteristic of Hollande. He stole from Mélenchon as well: the decision to design a completely fake popular movement, something that was supposed to be elaborated from the grassroots. But, he sensed that this was also something that was in the air and that he had to capture. And meanwhile, he is also a populist in the vulgar sense of the term.

TA: The government is a national government: socialists, conservatives. So, it is a government which we've seen before but now under a new president who doesn't belong to any party and can play the role of a petit Bonaparte, who can manoeuvre these people and do what he wants with them. So, how is he going to manage? More importantly what is he going to do?

OT: He wants 'flexible' labour laws. He wants to sack 120,000 public servants. He wants to make cuts worth €60 billion. Here is something very interesting; that, if you permit a small digression, when asked where he was going to make the €60 billion cuts, his response revealed everything you need to know about Macron, his real intellectual matrix is in corporations and management: 'I'm going to preside, I'm not going to govern, I'm going to do what a CEO does, set tasks to my team and it's up to them to find a solution.'

So, of course, the option that does not even register is that maybe the teams could come back saying, 'We cannot do €60 billion cuts, you know, actually we need more investment in public services.' But it's like in management, I set a task for you and you have to get it done. And, so, that's what he wants to do. He has a majority to do it. The old extreme centre and its media will back him. The question is will he be able to.

What's going to happen is that you have a programme that has very low popular support and that is most likely going to be carried forward anyway, and that is going [to] widen the huge gap between the French population and the political representation. I think the campaign and the constant idealization of Macron has not convinced a majority in France. On the contrary it has widened the gap between the media and the people, a gap that was huge in 2005 when the media campaigned really shamelessly for the 'yes' to the European Constitution.

What we are going to see is a population in need of representation and this is where we have to be. Mélenchon was constantly criticized for his extreme intransigence against any alliances for the legislative elections. We were not in mixing wine with water …

We have taken a big leap forward in refounding the French left and we appeal to everyone on the broad left to join our ranks and take the struggle against neoliberalism forward. The victory of Macron and the defeat of the left is also an opportunity. The results have vindicated our approach to politics. Macron's popularity is already declining and the need to challenge his policies on every possible level is overwhelming. Tax breaks for the rich will not solve the structural crisis that is crippling the political economy of the country.

9

Germany: Heartland of the Centre

Something is rotten in the state of Germany, literally and metaphorically. During the summer of 2017, in the lead-up to the general election in September, it appeared that bridges connecting Germany to the rest of the EU were simply falling apart; meanwhile others were awaiting repairs. During that period, a number of the key bridges crossing the Rhine were closed to HGV traffic. On 3 August 2017, the local government was forced to close the 100,000-vehicles-a-day bridge at Neuenkamp, connecting the Ruhr industrial zone to Holland. The ecology benefited, but it put German capitalists into a grumpy mood. Transport barons did not hide their fury at every piece of bad news, treating each headline as a 'wake-up call'. Politicians began to speak of the threat posed to jobs.

This was all proof that Germany, long presented to the world as a byword for efficiency, is confronting a huge crisis of infrastructure. Investment in the public sector has dropped from 5 per cent in 2005 to 2 per cent in 2016. In both town and country, the gap in investment in infrastructure and maintenance stands at €126 billion, of which €34 billion is the backlog on roads and €33 billion on schools alone.[1]

But this was not an issue in discussion during the summer. The two subjects that dominated the September 2017 election campaign were interrelated: refugees and the growing social inequality in the country as a whole but also between North and South. Angela Merkel's generous offer to take a million refugees in 2015 divided opinion in every German political party, except the blood-and-soil groupings old and new, who were united on opposing any more foreigners being allowed into the country. In the following two years, Merkel's impulsiveness was reined in by her own party after her ratings began to nosedive. She 'corrected' herself without capitulating completely to the wave of xenophobia that swept the country.

The figure of one million galvanized the new right-wing Alternative for German (AfD) and the more extreme groupuscules further to the right. German

---

1   Guy Chazan, 'Cracks Appear in Germany's Cash-Starved Infrastructure', *Financial Times*, 4 August 2017.

capitalism itself was less upset, seeing in the new arrivals a huge supply of non-unionized cheap labour that would be 'flexible' and ideal for the low-paid, part-time 'mini-job' market. Neoliberal political anthropologists noted that the Syrians were light-skinned (more so than some indigenous Germans), fair-haired and would be indistinguishable from most Germans after a couple of generations. Capital saw the new arrivals as helping to solve the problem of a declining population. Religious and cultural contradictions would slowly work themselves out.

The second election issue, social inequality, has been rising in Germany over a longer period. The divide is not as great as in France, Italy, Britain and the United States, where the German model remains something to be envied, but perceptions within the country itself have changed. Today, the top 10 per cent control the wealth and pass it on to their children, while the bottom 40 per cent have nothing. Industrial capitalists have produced plenty of millionaires, but billionaires are much fewer proportionately than in the United States. An important reason for this is the lack, till now, of a property bubble. Germany has the lowest home ownership rate in the EU: only 45 per cent of Germans own their own homes. The housing market ensures that rented accommodation is available and affordable, though this could change over the coming years. Already, the consequences of this can be seen in certain sectors. The German education system reveals a larger gap between children from wealthy and poor families than the other OECD countries; likewise in the health sector.[2]

The ever-opportunist leader of the SPD (Social Democrats), Martin Schulz, backed by the IMF, made this issue a central focus of his US-style campaign in the September elections. His slogan was 'Time for More Equality, Time for Martin Schulz.' This was a contradiction on every level, completely ignoring the responsibility of his party as a crucial pillar of the centre coalition that runs the country. Schulz and the IMF want more public investment, mainly as a booster to encourage private investment. But any policy designed to ensure more profits and tax breaks for private capital is unlikely to be popular in Germany and might well lead to the growth of strong anti-EU currents.

In contrast, the chancellor, Angela Merkel, blames regulation and too much planning for creating the bottleneck in dealing with the crisis in hand. It was as if to suggest that a hurriedly constructed or repaired bridge that collapses after she is out of office is not her problem. The 2017 election is unlikely to solve this problem, which is not confined to Germany alone. No structural reforms were put in place after the 2008 crash anywhere. And the cost of this failure is that the filthy rich get filthier and richer, with political consequences, some of which reduce

2   Stefan Wagstyl, 'The Hidden Divide in Germany', *Financial Times*, 18 August 2017.

liberals to tears: Trump and Brexit being the most prominent examples. Why should Germany be the exception
in Europe? The signs of decline are now visible. The
solutions on offer are makeshift and unconvincing. The
cracks are affecting much more than the social infrastructure of the country.

Vivid confirmation of all this came with the election
results. Germany was once again a 'normal' European
state with both wings of the extreme centre suffering huge
blows. The far-right AfD won 12.6 per cent of the votes
and will have a hundred MPs in the new Bundestag. The
SPD received a battering with its share of the vote dropping to 20.5 per cent. This was the price for staying in
bed with the CDU/CSU far too long, and a shaken SPD
leadership declared it would not remain in a coalition
with Merkel. Her party's vote fell as well – from 41.5 to
32.9 per cent – but the CDU/CSU retained its position as
the largest single party. As the neoliberal Greens obtained
8.9 per cent and the staunchly pro-capitalist FDP 10.7
per cent, the combination of the two could compose a
new centre, if less stable than its predecessor. Die Linke
went up a fraction to 9.2 per cent. Challenges face all the
parties.

As far as the AfD is concerned, with its former leader
Petry gone, the remaining moderates will be rapidly mar-
ginalized and Gauland, Höcke and the neofascist gang will
take charge. At least, that is the plan. They obtained 21
per cent in the former DDR regions and about 10 per cent

in the old Federal Republic. The important thing to note is that they will be hard interlocutors in parliament. The new 'Jamaica' coalition will not be as stable as the alliance with the SDP. There are differences and the right-wing triumph will make the situation within the centre much more volatile.

What of Die Linke? They maintained their strength, got more votes than the Greens, who are a solid party of the extreme centre (neoliberalism and war), but fought a miserable, low-profile campaign. Hardly any posters or slogans, no reference to class struggle. Sahra Wagenknecht's first reaction after the elections was to say, 'We did not understand the fears of *normal* people on the refugee question.' But a majority of the *normal* people voted Merkel again, despite her being branded as 'soft on refugees'. If Die Linke moves rightwards after this result, they will find it hard to distinguish themselves from their SDP friends. The second danger is that the AfD will operate as the real opposition, and if Die Linke remains semi-passive it will decline.

Postwar German history can be divided into a number of distinct phases: the Cold War division of the country, with economic recovery in the western sector and the Stalinization of the eastern sector. The one-party state satirically named the German Democratic Republic (DDR) in East Berlin, a Grand Centre coalition in Bonn. A political and cultural rebellion in 1968 led by students erupted in the West, and was followed soon afterwards by the emergence of armed struggle groups that mainly targeted US bases and officers as well as German businessmen. At their peak, they were supported by 25 per cent of the West German population, mainly the young born during or soon after the war and finding it difficult to have breakfast each morning with ex-SS and Wehrmacht officers. In the East, a workers' uprising in 1953, demanding democratic rights and an end to the police state but not capitalism, greeted the death of Stalin. It pre-empted Khrushchev's 'secret speech' at the Twentieth Party Congress in Moscow by a few years and led to growing intellectual dissidence. Finally came the reunification of the country and the emergence of a new Germany, still not fully sovereign, partially through choice and partially the result of uncontested US hegemony and military bases. And the unified nation was crowned the dominant nation state in Europe, upon which depends the future shape and direction of the EU.

Immediately after the Second World War, the Soviet Union, whose armies were decisive in defeating the Third Reich, suggested an alternative to the division of the country. Earlier at the Yalta Conference the leaders of the anti-German alliance – Roosevelt, Churchill, Stalin – had agreed on a permanently demilitarized but undivided Germany. Churchill, however, secretly ordered Field Marshal Montgomery 'to be careful in collecting the German arms, to stack them so that they could easily be issued again to the German soldiers whom we should have to work with if the Soviet advance continued'.[3] Stalin remained loyal to the Yalta agreement except where he could not control the revolutionary forces, as in Yugoslavia. Accordingly, the Soviet leader proposed a unified but neutral Germany. The Western powers and their principal collaborators in the occupied Reich disagreed.

Konrad Adenauer, the conservative leader working closely with the United States, rejected any proposal that suggested Austria as a model. For him, Austria was not a country but a *schweinerei* (pig sty). In this opinion, he was backed by the former generals of the Wehrmacht. One of them, Wilhelm Schmalz, former commander of the Hermann Goering Tank Division, suggested the creation of a fully integrated European army, not an amalgam of national contingents, to defend Western Europe against the Soviet Union. The creation of such a force, Schmalz argued, could be the first step towards a political integration of the continent.

In this way the former Wehrmacht generals moved from Hitler to Truman at a great speed.[4] West Germany

---

3 Arthur L. Smith, *Churchill's German Army: Wartime Strategy and Cold War Politics, 1943–1947* (Beverly Hills, 1977), pp. 11–12.

4 Field Marshal Von Paulus, who surrendered at Stalingrad, was the only senior military leader of the Third Reich who chose to live in Dresden and worked as head of the East German Institute for Military Research. He belonged to a middle-class family (his father was a treasurer), and this lack of Junker aristocratic connections prevented his recruitment to the navy.

was rapidly integrated ideologically, politically and militarily into the structures of a United States–led Europe. But Schmalz's notion of a European army was a nonstarter. The British and French still ran large empires at the time. And even after they were compelled to abandon them, they remained attached to their 'national contingents', as they do to this very day. A European army as the spine of a united Europe never materialized. The Germans were allowed to rebuild their own armed forces and European unity was pursued by economic means.

The German political theorist Wolfgang Streeck has argued (see the conversation with him below) that the West German state was the ideal site to construct a model political centre in which conservatives and social democrats would often rule together. The hope was that the turbulent and tormented past could be erased forever. The war had helped wipe out both the Prussian Junkers and the German communists, who ceased to be a strength in the west. So both centrist parties could govern without challenge from right or left.

Reunification, when it finally arrived in 1990, was both an opportunity and a challenge. Here German conservatism behaved very much like its postwar predecessor. The chancellor in the West, Helmut Kohl, was not as sharp as Adenauer, but was just as short-sighted. He was helped by the last general secretary of the Soviet Communist Party, Mikhail Gorbachev, who was so desirous of pleasing Reagan and Thatcher that he offered them the DDR on a plate as a gift, demanding nothing in return. At the very least he could have insisted on the dissolution of NATO as an essential precondition. All he was offered was a verbal promise by the US not to expand NATO eastwards, which was a pledge they had no intention of keeping.

After unification, Helmut Kohl treated East Germany as conquered territory. East German academics, many of whom were dissidents while remaining Marxists, were purged from the universities and other institutions. Historians were specially targeted, the assumption being that they were all party hacks or so tainted with Marxist dogma that their work was worthless. This was far from the case.

A recent book, *East German Historians Since Reunification*, the outcome of a conference in New York, highlights the impact of the purge. In one of the essays in the volume, 'The Revenge of the Krupps? Reflections on the End of GDR Historiography', William A. Pelz writes how after reunification 75 per cent of East German academics were fired and, by 1998, of the 1,878 professors working in the Eastern German districts just over a hundred were from the East. West German ideologues and academics made no secret of the reasons for the political cleansing. Anti-capitalist historical research was not a priority. Moreover a complex narrative story was reduced to the level of an American western: goodies and baddies. All who worked for the academy in East Germany were the baddies.[5]

---

5   Alex Fair-Schulz and Mario Kessler, eds, *East German Historians Since Reunification* (New York, 2017).

The West German ideology was accepted by a large majority of its citizens, its politicians and its media. The triumph produced what is now largely a bland, complacent and self-referential culture.[6] There were a few dissenters. Oskar Lafontaine was a strong critic of Anschlussian reunification. In 1998, when the SPD finally won a majority, he told an internal party conference that discrimination against East Germans was unacceptable, pointing out that for him, 'If I had to put three Germans on a pedestal they would be Goethe, Heine and Brecht', and going on to praise the work of artists and academics in the old DDR.

But German conservatism had left a deep imprint and neither the new chancellor, Gerhard Schroeder, nor the finance minister and party chairman, Lafontaine, could reverse the process. East Germany was deindustrialized and treated like an occupied country. When, during the election campaign, Schroeder had promised to halve the number of unemployed during his chancellorship, Lafontaine argued that the only way this could be done was by dumping the Stability Pact imposed by Bonn as the price for monetary union and increasing domestic consumption with left-Keynesian policies. Schroeder disagreed strongly and Lafontaine resigned, the only major leader of a European social democratic party to quit in defence of social democratic principles.

---

6   The striking exception has been Edgar Reitz' trilogy *Heimat*, the first and only successful cinematic attempt at a country study by a European filmmaker.

The turn towards an extreme centre had begun and the Green Party, in alliance with the SPD, moved further to the right. Abroad, the Green foreign minister, Joschka Fischer, a sixties ultra-left radical, became the shameless defender of US-led 'humanitarian interventions' in the Balkans and later Afghanistan. Thus he helped to erase memories of the large movements against the Vietnam War and the stationing of cruise missiles in Germany. Meanwhile, at home a neoliberal order was put in place. There were tax cuts for corporations but not their employees. Generosity for bankers, nothing for consumers. Unemployment remained at almost the same level. The net result of the neoliberal regressions did very little to enhance the economy.

There is little doubt that the SPD–Green 'dream coalition' would have lost the 2002 elections had it not been for Bush's decision to invade and occupy Iraq. German public opinion was against the adventure. Even the Christian Democrats found it difficult to back the Americans in what became a cruel, protracted occupation. Gerhard Schroeder declared that he would not take Germany to war even if the UN Security Council approved the action. Fischer was sidelined together with Germany's liberal militarist philosopher Jürgen Habermas, horrified by the thought that a German chancellor was recognizing the UNSC for what it was and remains. The anti-war turn was decisive. The SPD–Green majority was only 6,000 votes.

At home the newly elected coalition went for Agenda 2010, full-blown neoliberalism: reduction of unemployment benefits, raising the retirement age, outsourcing, deregulation, reduction of subsidies, extension of shopping hours, and so on. It was bonanza time for German CEOs and most of the press. Internationally, the *Economist* spoke for the global elites and gave its backing to the measures:

> Most analysts readily agree on what is wrong with the German economy. First and foremost, the labour market is far too sticky. Second, taxes and social-security contributions are too high and profits too low. Third, and not unconnected, social security payments, pensions and healthcare arrangements are too generous. And fourth, there is far too much red tape.[7]

Agenda 2010 turned out to be a damp squib: celebrated in the media bubble, the citizenry unenthusiastic, the economy unaffected. Growing anger at the base of the SPD led to small splits in the party in the Ruhr and other parts of West Germany, accompanied by trade union discontent. Neoliberalism was past its peak. The pendulum had already begun to move, albeit very slowly, in the other direction.

Long-standing SPD voters began to abandon their party, feeling that it had moved too far to the right.

---

7 Special report, 'Loosen Up or Lose Out', *Economist*, 5 December 2002.

Elsewhere Schroeder began to lose crucial provincial elections, including North-Rhine Westphalia. Deceived by huge media support, which later disappeared during the campaign, Schroeder opted for an early election by denouncing the CDU's projection of Angela Merkel as a German Thatcher, defended 'German inter-class solidarity' and lost narrowly. Merkel had no choice but to form a Grand Coalition with the SPD. Schroeder was replaced and accepted a top position with Gazprom, the state-controlled Russian energy giant, working on a pipeline approved by his own government shortly before he left office. The move was widely denounced as a conflict of interest. The 'equality-loving' Martin Schulz declined to comment.

The Coalition agreed on measures that would weaken labour and strengthen German capital. As Perry Anderson pointed out:

> Cheaper labour in the former DDR was soon overtaken by still lower wage costs in Eastern Europe, as the prospect and then reality of EU enlargement drew a growing volume of German investment into Slovakia, Hungary, the Czech Republic, Poland and elsewhere. Beyond these, in turn, lay outsourcing of plants to Asia, Latin America, the Middle East, driving the original wedge of unification yet further into the domestic economy, prising loose the labour market.
>
> The result was a steep decline, not just in the numerical strength of German trade unions – membership of the DGB

dropping from 11 million in 1991 to 7.7 million in 2003 – but in their ability to resist unrelenting pressures from German capital. Real wages fell for several successive years, giving German firms an ever sharper competitive edge in high-end international markets. By 2004, Germany was once more – as it had been in the seventies – the world's leading exporter of manufactures. Such success was built not on an outstanding performance in productivity – US gains were significantly greater in the same period – but on wage repression, as workers were forced to accept longer hours and less pay under threat of outsourcing, and domestic consumption remained flat. But with a swelling export surplus, investment increased and once the business cycle kicked up, growth at last accelerated in 2006, just as Merkel settled into office. By early 2008, unemployment had dropped by nearly two million. The serum of deregulation, injected from the East, seemed finally to have worked.[8]

The stock market crash that temporarily disoriented Western capitalism came two years into this process. The crash strengthened the critics of neoliberalism on left and right, described in the global media networks as 'populists'. This quickly became a code word for extremism and those who refused to worship the status quo, as Marco D'Eramo noted in his essay 'Populism and the New Oligarchy':

8   Perry Anderson, 'A New Germany?', *New Left Review* 57, May–June 2009, pp. 11–12.

The inflated use of the term 'populism' by the *optimates* thus reveals a covert anxiety. Just as the adulterous spouse is always the one most suspicious of their own partner, so those who eviscerate democracy are the most inclined to see threats to it everywhere. Hence all the to-do about populism betrays a sense of uneasiness, smacks of overkill. The faintest murmur of dissent is turned into an alarming sign, heralding the ominous rumble of thunder that threatens to erupt into the hushed salons of the powerful, who believe themselves safe, but still anxiously peep out from behind the curtains for any signs that the people may be stirring: '*Vade retro vulgus!*' Or as they say these days, 'Get back in line!'[9]

The first breach with the German extreme centre emerged on the left in 2005. Oskar Lafontaine, the staunch leader of left-wing refugees from the SPD and others in the West, merged his forces with Gregor Gysi's PDS (Party of Democratic Socialism), a successor to the party that had governed the DDR in the East, to form Die Linke (The Left), uniting socialists in both parts of Germany against the centre. Since then the party has enjoyed moderate success, helped by the Greens' shift to the right. But its weakness has been an overeagerness to enter into coalitions with the SPD on a local level that resulted in the loss of significant local support in Berlin.

Die Linke did well in the 2009–10 regional elections,

9   Marco D'Eramo, 'Populism and the New Oligarchy', *New Left Review* 82, July–August 2013, pp. 27–8.

boosting its 'parliamentarism from below' strategy, and swallowed up more than a few leading activists. However, as a result, the dialectic of partial conquests, strongly opposed by Lenin in 1917, has now affected many left parliamentary parties. Expressed simply, once gains have been made (such as winning new members of parliament and running provincial governments), the party avoids taking political risks that might threaten the loss of even the smallest advantages it has won. Die Linke now confronts the same dilemma.

Till now the refusal of Die Linke to support NATO has made it untouchable as a coalition partner for the SPD on a national level. And there is evidence that some of its support has shifted to the right: in 2016, Die Linke had 60,000 registered members, down from 78,000 in 2009. A small proportion (10 per cent) is under thirty and 20 per cent are classified as workers. The party is effectively a radical-left social democratic party that has, to its credit, created a new intellectual space via the Rosa Luxemburg Stiftung (RLS), recalling Brecht's dictum that 'thinking is the most useful and pleasurable of activities'.

Critical scholarship is not confined to grants from the RLS, however. The German academy, largely conformist and passive, still manages to produce intellectual scholars of a very high quality. Wolfgang Streeck, a son of German refugees fleeing Eastern Europe after the war, is one such person. He taught sociology and industrial relations at the University of Wisconsin–Madison in the late eighties, returning to Germany in 1995 to take up the post of director of the Max Planck Institute for the Study of Societies and working as professor of sociology at the University of Cologne. He retired from his directorship in 2014, becoming emeritus director, a role that gave him the time to produce a series of important books on the political economy of capitalism and a constructive but sharp critique of the existing EU. The conversation below took place in 2016:

TARIQ ALI: What I want to talk to you about is Germany, its position in Europe after the reunification. It was unhappy for the East Germans on many levels, especially I felt, not so much economically because even the unemployment benefits they got were not bad compared to the past, rather good in fact, but psychologically and politically they felt like they were being treated as inferior. Has this stopped?

WOLFGANG STREECK: No, interestingly, it's now more politically significant than it was in the past. After 1990, they were showered with all sorts of benefits, like currency union. The entire West German Social Welfare System was moved in one big step to East Germany.

That was quite remarkable. I've done some research on this, and talked to some of the major players at the time. Helmut Kohl was about to reform at the end of the 1980s in a major, neoliberal way, including blows against the German welfare state. Then came unification and, in order to get unification accepted, he had to make an alliance with the social policy advocates. The deal meant that we won't do two things at the same time. We can't touch the welfare state and do unification at the same time. The agreement was to make a smooth economic unification the major priority.

It was only after a number of years that people in East Germany began to see that the price they paid for unification was a very high level of unemployment. At the end of the 1990s we had a level of 20 to 25 per cent unemployment in East Germany. That began to stick, and when Agenda 2010, the 'reform programme' of Schroeder, passed in 2000 – essentially a fiscal measure to deal with the economic costs of East Germany – the 'Easties' began to become more rebellious politically and psychologically.

Up to the present day, per capita income in East Germany has been 80 per cent of the national average. But Germany has for years moved roughly 4 to 5 per cent of its gross domestic product every year, to subsidise East Germany. It's a lot of money. We're still paying the so-called solidarity tax, in order to fund this subsidy.

An interesting comparison is with Italy, between the North and Southern Italy, which functions in exactly the same way as Germany. There is resentment brewing, among the richer parts of the country, against the continuous transfers; while at the same time the recipients of the transfers are not happy with them. They don't see much progress, and at the same time they feel that they are being treated from above as welfare recipients, which violates their pride.

TA: What is your assessment of German politics today? We have had almost continuously a 'grand coalition' government, which is an institutionalized centre government that agrees a consensus, to which they've kept. The Social Democrats and the Christian Democrats are one government. Is this going to continue indefinitely? Or can the Social Democrats break from this pattern and move in some other direction?

WS: I don't think we can make any guesses about the future these days because it's such a turbulent situation. Anything can happen. Germany is a country of grand coalitions, but even when only one party is in government, and the other is in opposition, they agree on many, many things. That is roughly the same, I think, as it was in England under Blair, where the Conservatives had a hard time saying where they differed. And the reason why this is the case is that we had considerable polarization between the parties in the 1970s. Unification forced them together.

In any case, you have to add that we have a federal structure. Very often, the second chamber – which is very important, much more important than the House of Lords – is in the hands of regional government, dominated by the other big party. When the federal government is controlled by the Christian Democrats, then you often have a majority in the second chamber of Social Democrats. There is an inbuilt necessity for some form of a coalition that is unnecessary in the Westminster-style democracy. In Germany a coalition in good times makes every policy decision predictable. In bad times it makes for a lack of flexibility, originality, and so on.

TA: But Germany, by and large, with the exception of the reunification, has been run quite smoothly by its ruling class until now. Now, even before the crisis over the refugees, there was real unease within the SPD and we saw the emergence and rise of Die Linke, a coalition between left Social Democrats in West Germany, led by Oskar Lafontaine, and former communists in East Germany and maybe new people who belonged to neither. The growth of the extremist right and the Alternative for Germany (AFG) suddenly took everyone by surprise, so that we then wondered what the hell was going on. Suddenly, the rough edges are beginning to show just like in other parts of Europe. Why is this happening? Is it simply the refugees or immigration, two related but different problems, or is it something else as well?

WS: Of course there are some commonalities and there is specificity. We have seen this in all the major Western democracies as a result of the opening-up of these societies, the globalization process, free trade, and so on. We see resistance among the losers of globalization in cultural terms as well as in economic terms and an increase in electoral turnout as a result of dissatisfaction accumulating in certain regions. There is something specific about the German situation, which is this big taboo about the nation. To simplify a little bit, the German cultural consensus after the Second World War was that there is not supposed to be a German nation. Germany is disappearing into a united Europe. And the ideal position would be for nations in general to lose their significance.

In a sort of way it is sometimes like the joke: 'If you meet someone outside Germany and you want to find out where he comes from, and you ask where he comes from, and he says, "I'm a European," then you know he's a German because nobody else would say that.' One would say, 'I'm from England' or 'I'm from France' but a German will say, 'I'm from Europe.' But this is in a sense a denial of national history and the national character. Now, after unification, this became more difficult.

TA: I would have thought that it's virtually impossible now to remain in denial.

WS: Yeah, it is but cultural discourse is a very different thing from reality. An intellectual like Jürgen Habermas, at the time of unification, argued that the Germans hadn't deserved unification and that it was deplorable that they were setting up a commissariat and that now, even more than before, Germany had to be integrated into a united Europe otherwise it could never be trusted. Günter Grass had the same idea in 1990. Many Germans feel ambivalent about their own nationality, especially after unification. I remember the people becoming very squeamish when, after the Leipzig demonstrations in favour of German unity, they displayed posters saying, '*Wir sind das Volk*,' (we are the people). That was still just about okay but the following Monday the posters said, '*Wir sind ein Volk*' (we are one people). This was seen as politically incorrect in the eyes of the West German intelligentsia because the first poster emphasized *das Deutsche Volk* – the German people.

TA: The Marlene Dietrich philosophy: *never again Germany*.

ws: Yes, that is absolutely true. In fact there is a movement of young people in Germany that call themselves *Nie wieder Deutschland*: Never again Germany.

TA: One can admire them for thinking like this, but it's completely unrealistic.

ws: It is completely unrealistic. If you declare yourself a non-German and European everybody else will recognize you as a German. I lived in the United States for ten years and I know that nations are the place where people are formed. They are recognized on this basis and you have to live with your own nationality as well as your own national history. Now, in Germany today, in the received political doctrine, the idea of national interests is something you don't even talk about.

The important thing in the German ideology is the way German politicians define national interests as a shared European interest. So the German state has no national interests. Europe has interests. We try to work for those. Now, an interesting thing is that if you move around Europe and talk to people you see that this idea of the Europeanization of Germany, or the Europeanization of the German national interest, is sometimes received as a threat. As the Germanization of Europe: the German interest masquerading as the European.

And, of course, in everyday political discourse, people unintentionally do that. For example, our currency ... Everybody else sees austerity as a sort of cold-hearted, cold-blooded interest-driven German economic policy in the service of the German exports. It's very hard to explain to Germans that others see it like this because they think the economic recipes that they have for their own economy, since they work in their own economy, must work for everybody else. And, of course, it's not the case, but then economists have an answer to this. They say it's not enough, or the medicine has to be increased in dosage, you have to have more of the bitter medicine if it doesn't work.

TA: When do you think this ostrich-like notion that the Germans have to keep themselves in the background and try and hide who they are is going to end? I mean, it just defies history, it defies economics, and politics today. It's helped by the fact that German foreign policy, except on Iraq and one or two things which were very positive, is still very much dominated by Atlanticism. And so nothing can be done that is independent-minded, either for Europe or for Germany.

WS: It would require a total rethink of German foreign policy orthodoxy, which would represent a huge shift. Perhaps Trump will force them to do so.

Helmut Schmidt, during a very bright moment once said that 'the problem of Germany located in the centre of Europe is that we are too big to be loved and too small to be feared'. And that encapsulates something very important. We cannot govern the continent because we're too small. At the same time, unlike the Dutch or the Danes, we cannot be everybody's darling because we're too big. German foreign policy will always have to work in this niche.

TA: But that is exactly what the aim of the Third Reich was on this continent. Carl Schmitt argued it very clearly: we want to have the same sphere of influence in Europe that the United States has in South America.

ws: One problem facing German imperialism in the 1930s and 1940s was, again, this problem of size. We had an over-sized manufacturing industry that depends on access to foreign markets. We also needed to buy the raw materials for this from foreign markets. So, the fear of the Germans in the 1920s and, in fact, before the First World War, was that other powers, in particular the British Empire, might cut them out of those markets, severely restricting the German economy. The Nazis answered this question by inventing the doctrine of autarchy. You have to militarily conquer, occupy and, then, draw a boundary around an extended Germany, one that had markets as well as raw materials.

After the Second World War, that problem was – and you mentioned the long peace – solved in a number of ways, partly because Germany was cut into three or four pieces, partly because it had to be integrated into the West, and due to the Cold War. But the most important part was that, unlike in the 1920s, a way was found to guarantee Germany access to foreign markets, both for its industrial product and for the provision of raw materials. And this was via the free trade zone of Europe. So it solved a problem that German imperialism had tried to solve. This was tremendous historical progress and extremely important for Germany. That is why the idea of continental integration is so fundamental to German foreign policy thinking.

Now it has taken the form of the euro, which I think needs to be fundamentally revised because, unlike in the

1950s, German integration into Europe is not Germany becoming part of Europe but the Mediterranean countries and others are becoming extended EU colonies.

We need to find a construction in which we don't govern, but rather cooperate. It has to be cooperation because it cannot be imperialism. But at the same time without cooperation we're done for. And that's a core problem. If you want to understand the postwar development of West Germany there are two key points that need to be grasped.

First among the events that put West Germany on the path to what it would later become was the arrival of 10 million refugees from the East, who made up roughly one in five inhabitants of a devastated territory less than half the size of the pre-war Reich. While some of them remained isolated, depressed and poor for the rest of their lives, others brought with them a determination to fit in and succeed in what was for them in many ways a foreign country. Their arrival disrupted forever the fabric of what had been until then a largely traditional society divided between urban and rural, Catholic and Protestant, left and right. Centuries-old parochial ways of life and socio-cultural milieux were broken up, often in the face of adamant resistance. But, ultimately, the skills and hard work of the newcomers contributed to their new homeland. This forced the locals to give them a chance to establish themselves. As a result, West Germany became a uniquely competitive and meritocratic society.

Secondly, as Ralf Dahrendorf was probably the first to recognize, the two forces that had between them worn down the Weimar Republic – the eastern aristocracy (the Junkers, whom Max Weber had identified as the Reich's main roadblock to capitalist modernity) and the communist opposition – had disappeared. The Junkers had been decimated by the Nazis after the putsch of 1944, and the rest were killed or driven from their estates by the advancing Red Army. The communists now had their own state under Soviet sponsorship, the German Democratic Republic, which weakened them in the West so that in 1956 the West German Constitutional Court outlawed the party.

Both wings, reactionary and potentially progressive, of onetime resistance to capital were thus eliminated, leaving only the Social Democrats (SPD) and Christian Democrats (CDU) in the middle. The CDU, a descendant of the Catholic Zentrumspartei of the Weimar period, appealed to Christians irrespective of denomination, in keeping with the postwar break-up of homogeneous local confessional communities. Add to this the disappearance of the Nazis as an organized political force and the incarceration of Germany's industrial tycoons by the Allies (albeit soon to be released to help with the Korean War). The result was a vastly simplified political landscape and an economic geography shorn of the parasitic manorialism of Prussia, now dominated instead by what would become the highly productive dualism of a small-firm economy in the south, south-west and Rhineland, and the huge industrial complexes in the Ruhr.

TA: Given the debate on refugees (in this case, of course, non-German), it's interesting the importance you attach to them as a dynamic force in the revival of the economy.

WS: You can appreciate what it means: 12 million people, who had been driven out of their homes [after the war] and who had to make it in this society. There was a sense of competitiveness, of the need for hard work. But you can imagine these new people. They were all over the place. The old divisions between Catholic and Protestant areas were completely wiped out. In Bavaria suddenly you had Protestants; in Northern Germany you had Catholics. Basically, these people had to settle down where the trains ended.

In the history of my family, I was born in refugee housing in Northern Germany. My father was from Pomerania, my mother from what is now the Czech Republic. After 1945, they were told to leave within forty-eight hours with whatever they could carry. And now they arrive in this place, they know nobody. My parents were not very educated people, and imagine 10 million people like this.

This inserts dynamism in a society and removes all traditional safeguards against competition, against markets, and so on. No other European country had to undergo

275

this sort of shock treatment. But what it did was it opened up the political economy for a push into modernity or into modern capitalism in a way that no other country had to undergo.

TA: How would you best state your position on what is happening to capitalism today? Especially after 2008 and the crash of Wall Street but actually even before that the system was running out of steam, you've written, could you tell us why?

WS: The coexistence of capitalism and democracy was always precarious. Now in the last, let's say, eight to ten years I observe that the public language is becoming rougher. People are speaking up in ways that is outside of the cultural consensus and it takes up issues that all have to do with a desire to be protected from excessive or excessively fast social and political and economic change. This need for protection articulates itself today, and I think rightly so, in terms of a very important question: what is the function of borders of national economies and national societies? To what extent is it a moral obligation to have free trade? Or is it not rather also a political necessity to ensure that people who live in a given country and who have made commitments to themselves, to their family, to their occupation are not overrun by change?

So that, at the least, the opening of national societies

needs to be managed in a way that protects vested interests of people who do not live in the City of London and cannot get a job easily in Hong Kong if their job in London disappears. And what you see in our societies, and I can say this even applies to Germany, is that this division over what are boundaries good for becomes geographically visible in terms of the global cities and the would-be global cities of these countries being inhabited by people who look at the global system and see themselves as citizens of the world. Whereas the countryside and the small towns are inhabited by people who are afraid of change coming too fast and who are invested in local culture – as are the cosmopolitans of the central cities, only they don't know that they live in a local culture.

I'll give you an interesting example from Germany. The new right-wing party, the AfD, have their strongest support in the former East Germany. How is that possible? If you go to East Germany and talk to people who have grown up there, even younger people, they say that their sense of identification with their own biography is being continuously violated by a public discourse that declares them to be sort of backwards.

TA: Let's discuss something that is very related: the relationship between the European Union and the individual democratic states. The Maastricht Treaty of 1992 destroyed any hope of there being a democratic system in the European Union. And while some people make a big fuss about the European Parliament, actually, it's a body without too many powers. How do you explain this?

ws: There are different ways of approaching this. I think on the surface it is true that nations are historical constructions that do not easily disappear. And simply deciding that from now on we're no longer French, Frenchmen, Frenchwomen, we're now Europeans and everybody else becomes European is a voluntaristic view of politics that cannot work. Or even of social integration that cannot work.

I'm a sociologist; I have done a lot of comparative work. In order to understand a country that is not your own country you have to work very hard. There are background understandings, silent assumptions, communities of assumptions that are very difficult to explore for an outsider. Now, all of these understandings inform our political behaviour. So the French see the world in many ways – culturally, politically – differently from the Germans. Now, it is not in their genes and it may disappear, but it doesn't disappear in a matter of a decade or two.

If you look at the United Kingdom, the Irish, the English and the Scottish see the world in many ways. They have different historical grievances that you can't easily talk them out of. Now that doesn't mean that they can't live together in peace. But in order to have institutions to make this possible, you have to think about [those differences]. In other words, international politics, even on a small continent like Europe, cannot be completely submerged into the domestic politics of a big union.

I'm interested also in the economic part. The fundamental problem of the European Monetary Union, as we observe it now, can be briefly described. Capitalism as an economic system is designed to reorganize the societies it penetrates. These societies resist certain aspects of the commodification process that we call capitalist development. So there are different historical compromises between the capitalist market and the way society lives in families, in regional units, in local communities, and so on. You can also say this is a compromise between the modernity of capitalism and the traditionalism of societies. Responding to these different forms of the modern are counter-movements, like trade unions, political parties, and so on. So you have this tripartite division of society – traditional structures, capitalism, and modern anti-capitalist or revisionist structures.

In each of our countries this has been balanced out in different ways through long historical experiences. So, for example, French society is held together by the French state. There's no country where the state is more important than in France. The state is – has become – the driving force of, you can say, the compromise between society and capitalism. Italy had a similar way of settling the distribution of conflicts. The Germans are unique in the sense that their social compromise thrives on low inflation, because Germany is a manufacturing country and is a country that depends on exports. So in Germany, unions, employers, everybody, insists on low inflation. Now put these together in one currency union and it cannot work because you have to have different monetary policies to respond to the different institutional and political settlements between the political economies of these nations. A nation is an organization but organizations have been made historically and they cannot be unmade simply by fear.

TA: Or not just by fear but also by imagining that creating a currency for a whole continent, despite differences in language and in state structures, was ever going to work.

WS: In a way, the euro is the paradise for the German export industry, because you have fixed market access in Europe and the presence of the Italians and the Spanish and everybody else in the currency unit depresses the value of the currency. So why do the French and Italians want to remain in the euro?

The Irish are a little bit different, but as far as the Mediterranean countries are concerned I'm now convinced after some research that the intention was to import from Germany the hard currency, the euro, as a whip on their own societies – to break through the traditionalist residues of the old way of settling the relationship with capitalism in a way that I call 'a rationalization of the social structure'. This made it as historically pliable to capitalism as the German structure has become after 1945. The euro was a huge social experiment. It was an attempt 'to modernize' (I would say 'to rationalize') the social structure of the Mediterranean countries to become properly capitalized.

TA: What is the solution to the problems now posed by the EU, its structures, its functioning?

WS: We're now seeing a few things that begin to point in the right direction. And this is something where I give credit to Brexit, and to those that voted for it. Now, even Angela Merkel is beginning to understand that Europe cannot be a superstate. And that, more than that, Europe cannot be unified in one encompassing identical pattern for all countries of Europe. There has to be a different approach that recognizes the differences in interest and in structure and in history of the countries of Europe. We need close cooperation, there's no doubt about it, but we cannot have this cooperation being governed out of Brussels. This is beginning to trickle down. The Brexit was an important lesson.

TA: A huge blow?

WS: Yes. It forced them to think about it and, if I want to be constructive for a change, I would say that if Europe reforms itself on this pattern, then I could imagine a sort of association between Europe and Britain that would give both of them what they need, namely cooperation plus autonomy. But now if you want to apply this to European integration you also have to apply it to the currency union: it has to be broken up in one way or another. Now that doesn't mean that each of these countries will need to go back to national currencies and then survive in the world.

TA: So you think that Brexit and the fact that there are large anti-EU currents in most of the EU states is forcing a rethink?

WS: Yeah, I hope it will. There's no limit to the stubbornness and, in many ways, the stupidity of fifteen heads of government sitting in the same room. But there could be a possibility to learn something from this. In terms of the compromise between society and capitalism it has to be very much decentralized. People have to work out their ways of life in a commune with their own experiences, their own historical tools, and so on. That requires that the free trade imperative is severely qualified. You cannot have, for example, the thirty-five-hour week in France defended while at the same time you open up your entire economy to the outside world. That is not possible. Nations like the Danes understand this, the Swedes understand this; people must learn – this needs to be understood.

In other words, when talking about democracy, you need to talk about the anchoring of institutions that modify markets and protect social life from capitalist dynamism. The anchoring of these institutions in the social structure is not the same all over Europe. In other words, you need different devices. In order for these different devices to be effective you need to protect them somehow against external interference. I know this is in many ways utopian, but since we're talking about democracy, this is one of the things that need to be kept in mind otherwise there can be no democracy.

Afterword

Alternatives

Bertolt Brecht, who understood better than most what it was like to live in a period of defeat, was equally aware of the brittleness of victories. One of his last poems, 'Counter-Song', fits well in our time:

> So does that mean we've got to rest contented
> And say, 'That's how it is and always must be,'
> And spurn the brimming glass for what's been emptied
> Because we've heard it's better to go thirsty?
>
> So does that mean we've got to sit here shivering
> Since uninvited guests are not admitted
> And wait while those on top go on considering
> What pains and joys we are to be permitted?

Better, we think, would be to rise in anger

And never go without the slightest pleasure

And, warding off those who bring pain and hunger

Fix up the world to live in at our leisure.[1]

'Our leisure'? What was going through Brecht's mind at the time? Living in East Germany, he might have been, half-ironically, recalling the famous line from the *Critique of the Gotha Programme* depicting the society envisaged by Marx: 'From each according to his ability, to each according to his needs.' This was something that could only come about in societies of abundance, and, since the real needs of the majority could never be fulfilled by capitalism, was only imaginable after an upheaval that altered the system based on exploitation and profit. The oppressed would have to emancipate themselves via a revolution. Yet this did not happen in the United States, Britain, Japan and Germany, where productive forces were at their most advanced; instead revolutions occurred in Tsarist Russia and war-torn China, and later in Vietnam and semi-colonial Cuba.

The first three countries have since reverted to a hybrid capitalism that exhibits, in many ways, conditions similar to those prevailing in Victorian Britain or the Gilded Age in the United States. Aspects of life in Chinese cities

---

1   Bertolt Brecht, *Poems 1913–1956*, edited by John Willet and Ralph Mannheim, with the co-operation of Erich Fried (London and New York, 1976).

today are Dickensian, while the oligarchs of post-Soviet Russia have a lot in common with the leading criminal gangs that terrorized the East Coast and the Midwest of the United States in the late nineteenth and twentieth centuries. The process whereby such gangsters went 'legit' and integrated themselves within the system is currently underway in parts of Europe and Central Asia, reaching maturity in China.[2]

The uneven development of capitalism has deepened its contradictions. The astonishing development of technology, the third industrial revolution in the Western world and Japan, has undoubtedly created the material basis to satisfy the needs of all their citizens; but the economic structure based on maximizing profits at any cost is like a concrete wall that divides the top layers from the rest. The cost of production is now so low that the practical value of the commodity has to be ignored in order to keep prices artificially high. With the savage deindustrialization of the West, the parasitic marketing and advertising industries are among the largest in the world, second only to arms production. Consumerism has conquered all. Our needs are manipulated. Sixty-seven varieties of jeans, washing powders organic and non-organic, hi-tech gadgets and thousands of other commodities large and

---

2   Crime and capitalism are old bedfellows, and as the latter became more and more sophisticated, so did the criminals. Today, in order to be a truly successful criminal, you have to be inside the system or a top-grade hacker.

small, most of them unnecessary. Who decides? The market, chorus the neoliberals. But the market itself is controlled by the ruling elites, via a set of mechanisms such as the acceleration of inbuilt obsolescence.

There is nothing neutral about the market. Its devotees increasingly resemble primitive cults, with this difference: the more intelligent capitalists know full well that the system is doomed, but they also know, and it is what gives them enormous confidence, that the state will scupper any attempt to overturn the system. The favoured method these days consists in pre-emptive strikes where necessary (repression) accompanied by Project Fear (psychological and media blitz). It would be naïve in the extreme to imagine that the surveillance regimes in force in the US and the EU are directed exclusively against 'terrorism' and its perpetrators.

As is now public knowledge, the NSA and its counterparts in other countries spy on economic rivals who may be official 'friends' (the friend/enemy dichotomy is a list regularly updated), and also on their own citizens. Hackers are frequent targets, not just those designated as 'cyber-terrorists' whose ability to cancel bills, debts or overdrafts makes them dangerous, but also many others who will not submit to, or spy for, the system. More fundamental is the capacity of some hackers to challenge the entire ethos of capitalism by making virtually everything (except the computer) free: Linux and copyleft (counterposed to copyright) are the shining example. The inventor of Linux was a twenty-two-year-old Finnish hacker, Linus Torvalds. Unlike the stereotype, Torvalds worked in tandem with other hackers to construct a core that was easy for others to test and debug. He only built 2 per cent of it; 98 per cent was developed by his co-workers, and for free.

What they achieved was a rehearsal for how society as a whole could function without either capitalism as we experience it or the dictatorships that once dominated Eastern Europe and the Soviet Union. The technological revolution that erupted on the West Coast of the US has, in effect, made possible a complete overhaul of individual and social relations.

Who can make it happen? Movements from below are a necessary starting point for any change. It is action, experience of struggle, partial victories, defeats, overcoming them (often in unpredictable fashion) and triumphs small and large that crystallizes ideas, especially radical ideas, which are typically submerged by the weight of the present in times of normal conservatism or violent reaction. Mass movements blow away the borders of existing consciousness and revive or recreate radical politics. The process is multiform, depending on the history and political culture of each country. Attempts to mimic a success elsewhere usually result in defeats. The Russian Revolution of 1917 was the outcome of an inter-imperialist war and the peculiar conditions of Tsarist Russia, completely different from those of Weimar Germany and the rest of Western

Europe. Ill-thought-out, if noble, uprisings in Germany, seeking to break the isolation of the Bolsheviks, ended in failure – with the loss of the finest flowers of German socialist thought. Fear of more such upheavals paved the way for the defection of the bourgeoisie and landed gentry to fascism, first in Italy and later in Germany.

The triumph of the Cuban Revolution in 1959 created a wave of passion and enthusiasm throughout Latin America, and many believed that the same methods would obtain the same success elsewhere. Once again the finest militants were exterminated by repressive regimes backed to the hilt by the US, financially, militarily and politically. The CIA torturers cloned themselves throughout the continent, and created a special School for Torturers (aka the School of the Americas) for the purpose.

In Europe and Asia, the left fell into complete disarray after 1989, as the collapse of the Soviet Union was coupled with the economic rise of China, once the CCP and its state had embraced the latest version of capitalism. By contrast, despite certain problems, the Cuban Revolution and its legacy remained a source of inspiration for much of the Latin American left, long after the phase of continental guerrilla warfare had come to an end. In a period when all seemed lost, events in South America took the world by surprise.[3]

---

3   For more detailed accounts, see Tariq Ali, *Pirates of the Caribbean: Axis of Hope* (London and New York, 2006); Richard Gott, *Hugo Chávez* (London and New York, 2005); Gregory Wilpert,

Renewing the ideas of Simón Bolívar two centuries after his demise, the elected leader of Venezuela, Hugo Chávez, began to argue for continental unity against the Empire. The victories of Evo Morales in Bolivia and Rafael Correa in Ecuador and, to a lesser extent, the triumph of Lula in Brazil reignited hope across the continent and elsewhere. All four leaders visited Cuba several times for tutorials from their mentor. The old man in Havana, delighted by their success, warned against any ultra-left adventures and advised a cautious approach. After long decades of struggle and numerous defeats in South America, the isolation of the Cuban revolution had finally ended.

The Bolivarian leaderships in South America came to power democratically. They were backed by indigenous mass movements, but strongly opposed by the US–EU powers and the media barons of South America. They confronted a world in which any strict regulation of foreign or local capitalism was regarded as unacceptable and 'anti-democratic', while the increasing poverty and inequality inherent in capitalist societies was seen as a systemic necessity. For its latter-day defenders, capitalism has to be immunized against democracy. Repeated attempts to destabilize and topple democratic, anti-capitalist Bolivarian governments continue. The contrast

---

Changing Venezuela by Taking Power (London and New York, 2007); David Smilde and Daniel Hellinger, eds, *Venezuela's Bolivarian Democracy* (Durham, NC, 2011).

between the social democratic experiments of this *sui generis* left and the plight of Europe could not be greater. Might the disease spread?

For almost two decades I've argued that the Bolivarian experience, though it is far from perfect, offers a much better model for Europe and other parts of the world than neoliberalism. The capitalist system had turned the working and unemployed poor into exiles in their own countries. The huge social movements against privatizations and social restructuring in Venezuela (IMF impositions), Bolivia (water) and Peru (electricity) challenged this relegation and helped launch political parties which they then lifted into government. The movements had already pledged a series of anti-capitalist structural reforms to transform conditions. It was their successes in this field that enabled their repeated electoral triumphs.

This process had no equivalent in Europe. Here, deindustrialization had broken the spinal cord of the old working classes. Neoliberal impositions completed the process. Defeated and demoralized, the official trade unions, linked to a segment of the extreme centre, capitulated to neoliberalism. Their protest now tends to be confined to ritual marches or one-day strikes that have virtually nil impact, ignored by both the rulers and the new generation of semi-employed or unemployed youth who want change but feel that none of the traditional parties can provide it. The failure of established parties and the

non-existence of a left that is neither tainted by collabora-
tion with the extreme centre nor sectarian, has sent many
young people to the extreme right: France and Holland,
Hungary and the Baltic states remain the most striking
examples. In Italy, the social movements born out of anti-
capitalist and anti-imperialist struggles disappeared, after
the far-left groups they had supported joined extreme-
centre coalitions.

The crash of 2008 shook the system to its core. In order
to prevent economic life from falling apart, the state in the
US and the EU promptly bailed out the failing banks to
the tune of billions of dollars. Initially a paralysis gripped
these countries: the absence of any progressive alternative became painfully visible, as a handful of activists
targeted the homes of individual bankers and billionaires.
Even during its worst crisis, the ideology of neoliberalism
remained intact.

The decision to make the victims pay for a crisis that
had been caused by a deregulated banking system was too
much for the weakest links in the EU chain: Greece collapsed, followed by Portugal, Ireland and, later, Spain.
The extreme-centre parties in both Greece and Spain tottered and fell. The neoliberal turn in Greece had come
later than in other countries, but when it did it was spear-
headed by Costas Simitis, the Socialist (PASOK) prime
minister in 1996.[4]

---

4   'It was Costas Simitis, PASOK [Socialist] prime minister from
1996 to 2004, aided by Papademos at the central bank, who set the

A small socialist coalition of left groups, Syriza, suddenly became the main challenger to the extreme centre and came within a whisker (2.8 per cent margin) of winning the 2012 general elections. PASOK, the left segment of the centre, went into meltdown. As its support drained away and its parliamentarians returned to their homes, they were spat upon by angry constituents for having caved in to the draconian demands of the Troika. But in the process, Syriza had become a mass party, its leader, Alexis Tsipras, the new bogeyman of Europe – and not simply because he publicly declared that the person in world politics that he admired the most was Hugo Chávez. The South American model appeared to be heading towards Europe.

As a result, Project Fear was launched by the EU

country on a course of sell-offs and deregulation, while also claiming to cut the deficit, lower labour costs and crush inflation, bringing the country into line with EMU convergence criteria and joining the euro in 2001. Financial deregulation had produced a frenzy of speculative activity, boosting the Athens stock market to unprecedented heights and transferring large quantities of wealth upwards to a newly financialized elite; euphoria rose higher still in the run-up to the 2004 Athens Olympics. In reality, as the world now knows, the deficit figures were rigged: Simitis and Papademos oversaw a fee of $300 million to Goldman Sachs to shift billions of euros of debt off the public accounts. Yet even when this was revealed by Eurostat in 2004, the ratings agencies continued to give Greek bonds a triple-A investment grade.' Stathis Kouvelakis, 'The Greek Cauldron', *New Left Review* 72, November–December 2011.

leaders against Syriza, and it worked. The older segment of the population could not withstand the propaganda unleashed by the colossus. The EU bosses, aided by the newly elected French president, François Hollande, put the extreme centre back in power, but the coalition began to fray at its edges. Smaller parties, nervous of total wipeout, broke with the Conservatives but kept them in government. Syriza won the largest number of seats in the European elections soon after, and, if the polls are to be believed, will be the largest parliamentary party in the 2016 general elections.

Spain was once greatly admired by the Western media for its gutsy building industry and booming economy, a mighty bull that shamed the moping lions of 'Old Europe'. The crash of 2008 put an end to all that. As the housing market went under, unemployment jumped to 20 per cent and youth unemployment to twice that rate, in a country with a population of 45 million. The extreme centre (in this case the Socialist Party or PSOE) implemented drastic 'austerity' measures and tumbled to defeat. They were replaced by the Conservatives (Popular Party) that carried on their policies, albeit with a nastier rhetoric. A carefully orchestrated general strike in 2010 was used by union bureaucrats to win a few concessions, after which they happily signed a deal to cut back pensions and raise the retirement age. It was against this level of collabo-ration that radicalized Spanish youth – the *indignados* –

occupied the squares, making clear their disgust with traditional politics. Their anger was highly articulate. When a TV reporter pleaded with an *indignada* 'not to question democracy', Beatriz García's response was of epic proportions. She was not simply speaking for Spain, but arguing the case for change across the continent and beyond. Her words contained the embryo of a popular alternative, the basis for a new constitution, echoing the Bolivarians of South America:[5]

> Yes, we question this democracy because it fails to support popular sovereignty: the markets impose decisions for their own benefit and the parties in Parliament are not standing up to this global fact. Neither in our country nor in the European Parliament are they fighting to put an end to financial speculation, whether in currency or in sovereign debt.
>
> Yes, we question this democracy because the parties in power do not look out for the collective good, but for the good of the rich. Because they understand growth as the growth of businessmen's profits, not the growth of social justice, redistribution, public services, access to housing and other necessities.

---

5   The Bolivian president, Evo Morales, triumphed yet again in the 2014 elections in that country, winning a huge majority. The reasons are inscribed in the following figures: a doubling of the minimum wage, a quadrupling of taxes on oil companies, retirement age lowered to sixty, massive increases in spending on health and education, and the gearing of the latter to a broad and open conception of human intelligence.

Because the parties in power are concerned only for their continuation in office ... Because no politician has to live with what they legislate for their 'subjects': insecurity, mortgage debt, uncertainty. We question this democracy because it colludes with corruption, allowing politicians to hold a private post at the same time as public office, to profit from privileged information, to step into jobs as business advisors after leaving office, making it very profitable to be a politician.

Yes, we question this democracy because it consists in an absolute delegation of decision-making into the hands of politicians that are nominated in closed lists and to whom we have no access of any kind. Nor is there proportionality between votes and seats. We question this democracy because it is absurd that the only way to 'punish' a party is to vote for another one with which one does not agree. We question this democracy because the parties in power do not even comply with the social provisions of the Constitution: justice is not applied equally, there are no decent jobs or housing for all, foreign-born workers are not treated as citizens. Excuses are not good enough for us. We do not want to choose between actually existing democracy and the dictatorships of the past. We want a different life. Real democracy now!

Oh, the ironies of history. An already hollowed-out democracy, under further attack by neoliberal governments, is being defended by radical activists engaged in autonomous extra-parliamentary struggles for a better society. And as Greece and Spain demonstrate, the young political leaders of these movements are not without a hinterland. Both countries experienced brutal civil wars and dictatorships where Marxist, anarchist and social-ist ideas were outlawed, and leftist militants imprisoned, tortured, often killed. Their organizations were banned. Syriza's Alexis Tsipras was the head of a Communist youth organization in Greece. Pablo Iglesias evokes his own history to explain how Podemos determines its priorities:[6]

The 'Secret' of Podemos
According to Pablo Iglesias

I have defeat tattooed on my DNA. My great-uncle was shot dead. My grandfather was given the death sentence and spent five years in jail. My grandmothers suffered the humiliation of those defeated in the Civil War. My father was put in jail. My mother was politically active in the underground. My first experience of political socialization as a child was in the mobili-zations against NATO [in the eighties], which was the last time that the left in this country thought we could win. It upset me enormously to lose … And I've spent many years, with col-leagues, devoting almost all of our political activity to thinking how we can win …

The things I say in the mass media and how I say them require a great many hours' work where we think about how

6   The most useful analysis of the origins and political approach of Podemos can be found in a set of three essays by Luke Stobart on the Left Flank blog.

to move through an absolutely hostile terrain … We were in
Latin America and we watched and watched how they did
things there to win. And here is the secret. The first thing is not
to feel any fear … [Second,] I know that all left activists want
the whole of the left to be united … If all of the left organizations unite, then we can beat the rogues in charge.

Rubalcaba [the PSOE leader] and Rajoy [the PP president
of Spain] would love it if we didn't think like that, because they
know that then we would be limited to 15 or 20 per cent [of
the vote] … I don't want to be the 20 or 15 per cent. I don't
want my biggest political aspiration to be taking three regional
ministries from the Socialist Party. I don't want to be a 'hinge'.
I want to win. And in a context of complete ideological defeat
in which they have insulted and criminalized us, where they
control all of the media, the left needs to stop being a religion
and become a tool in the hands of the people if it is to win. It
needs to become the people …

I know that this pisses off people on the left. We like our
slogans, symbols and anthems. We like getting together as a
group. We think that if we get several party initials on a poster
this means we are going to win. No way. [Winning] is about
people's anger and hopes. It is about reaching people who
otherwise would see us as aliens, because the left has been
defeated …

What should democrats do? Democracy is taking power
off those that monopolize it and sharing it out among everyone, and anyone can understand that … 15-M sent a damned
message – firstly to the left, and there were left-wingers that

took it badly. I remember left leaders saying, 'I've been *indignado* [outraged] for thirty years. Are these kids going to come and tell me what being outraged is all about?' OK, but it wasn't you that brought together hundreds of thousands in the Puerta del Sol.

The fact that [15-M] attracted the largest mobilization since the NATO referendum, and that this has been able to change this country's political agenda to put the demand for democracy first, does that reveal [the left's] strength? No, it shows our damned weakness. If the unions and social organizations were organized, we wouldn't need things like [Podemos]. The problem is that in times of defeat, so you don't get defeated again ... you have to think and say 'we can be the majority'.

Politics is never absent, but the new politics on offer vary from country to country. Some of the young leaders of the Radical Independence Campaign in Scotland emerged from the implosion of British far-left groups; for them, casting off the shackles imposed by dogma and cult has been intellectually liberating, and has transformed their modus operandi. It is where the new movements have broken completely with the extreme centre that the successes have been most marked.

Elsewhere there is a great deal of confusion. In Germany, the Left Party – a hold-all for the remnants of the old East German Communist Party represented by the arch-opportunist Gregor Gysi, leftist social democratic breakaways from the SPD, symbolized by Oskar Lafontaine, radical Green refugees from the party of Joschka Fischer, and more – is on the decline. That is the price for refusing to break with the extreme centre and, in fact, collaborating with it on local and regional levels. The Gysi faction is desperate to merge with the SPD, and a recent *Financial Times* editorial suggested that it was time to stop demonizing the Left Party and bring it in from the cold. In return, Gysi would have to support NATO and imperial wars.

In Italy, the 2013 general election triumph of the stand-up comedian Beppe Grillo's Five Star Movement (M5S) startled the country, and sent the extreme-centre parties scurrying in all directions to see how the new threat could be defeated. Giorgio Napolitano, Italy's octogenarian president,[7] began to intrigue and manoeuvre to place Matteo Renzi, a young Democrat Party apparatchik from Florence, in power. Renzi was the third unelected prime minister installed by Napolitano. His ambition is to change the electoral law so that third parties are neutralized and winner takes all, like in Britain.

---

7   Napolitano, former leader of the Italian Communist Party, has been scathingly described as follows: 'An Italian Vicar of Bray, Napolitano had over a long career exhibited one fixed principle, adhesion to whatever world-political trend appeared to be a winner at the time … Once president, he went out of his way to ingratiate himself with Bush and Obama alike.' Perry Anderson, 'The Italian Disaster', *London Review of Books*, 22 May 2014.

These were ideal political conditions for a radical alternative. M5S, alas, showed no signs of moving in that direction. Its two principal leaders, Beppe Grillo and Gianroberto Casaleggio, hail from the entertainment and internet marketing industry respectively – very different backgrounds than their Greek and Spanish counterparts. While targeting political corruption quite effectively, their own manifesto for all seasons did not offer much hope. It was confused in the extreme, an unappealing mixture of neoliberalism and anti-capitalism. Small wonder that some of his Italian critics regard Grillo as a wasteful diversion. Others are less restrained. They point out that the M5S structure permits little room for dissent and is firmly controlled from the top. If so, there are bound to be explosions from within. The writers' collective Wu Ming are thoroughly sceptical, emphasizing that 'the M5S's mayor of Parma, Federico Pizzarotti … has been implementing austerity policies in Parma for months now, going back on his bombastic electoral promises, one after another.' For them, nonetheless,

A new phase is beginning now that 'Grillism' has entered parliament, chosen as a last resort by millions of people who found all other political options either disgusting or unworthy of a vote. The only way to interpret the phase that is just beginning is to understand the role that Grillo and Casaleggio played in the phase just ending. Many believe they acted as arsonists; we believe they were actually fire-fighters.[8]

8   Online at archivio.internazionale.it.

The contradictions within the organization, often suppressed, came to the fore soon after the tragedy in the first two weeks of October 2013, when almost four hundred migrants in unsafe boats, seeking refuge, drowned before they could land on the island of Lampedusa, one of the many frontiers of Fortress Europe. The Italian authorities let it happen. Similar disasters had been occurring on a lesser scale for the last quarter of a century, but this time the number of deaths, and the Pope's denunciation of what had happened as 'a disgrace', forced all the parties in Italy to take notice. As a consequence, for about fifteen minutes, the streets were flooded with crocodile tears. How would M5S react? Two of its senators, Maurizio Buccarella and Andrea Cioffi, spoke out strongly and followed this up on the Senate Justice Commission: they successfully moved an amendment to the most authoritarian clause of the Bossi-Fini Law, demoting unofficial migration from a criminal to an administrative offence.

Left critics of the M5S were not at all surprised by what happened next. The historian Toby Abse described what followed in graphic terms:

> The day after the M5S senators put themselves in the vanguard of parliamentary anti-racism, taking the initiative out of the hands of the PD and SEL, they found themselves the object of a thunderous denunciation by Beppe Grillo and Gianroberto Casaleggio (the co-founder of the M5S, who taught Grillo everything he knows about the internet), on Grillo's official

blog. The duo angrily explained: 'The M5S was not born to create Dr Strangeloves in parliament without control.' They continued: 'If we had proposed the measure during the general election campaign, the M5S would have obtained the percentages of a telephone prefix', inferring that almost all of their voters were not only racist, but saw immigration as the primary issue, which is hardly credible, even if a sizeable chunk of the M5S's northern electorate may have been drawn from disillusioned supporters of the Lega Nord, known as *leghisti*.

They followed this up with an appalling piece of right-wing populism: 'Substituting themselves for public opinion, for the popular will, is the common practice of the parties that want to "educate" the citizens, but it is not ours.' Besides, changing the law would be 'an invitation to migrants from Africa and the Middle East to set sail for Italy … How many illegals are we able to receive, if one Italian in eight does not have money to eat?'[9]

Grillo's anti-immigrant views are no secret. In 2011 he was quoted in the conservative press uttering remarks no different in tone and content to those of Britain's Ukip. The difference is this: Grillo *is* a clown, Farage merely pretends to be one. No surprise either that M5S sits with the right in the European Parliament. *Il Fatto Quotidiano*, the daily that waged a very strong campaign against

---

9   Online at weeklyworker.co.uk.

the corruptions of the Italian extreme centre, was once a staunch supporter of Grillo. It, too, has begun to take a distance.

The attempts to roll back neoliberalism are gathering momentum, but what to put in its place, and by what means, remain subjects for debate. The most successful movements are targeting the political structures of the state. Taking on its socio-economic base and transforming it on the South American model – state ownership of utilities and heavy regulation of capital – is an essential next step. This will not be easy in Europe. The power of the world financial system, both officially and through rogue elements, to try and paralyse an economy has been on display in several recent cases. They include Argentina, attacked by a vulture fund based in the Cayman Islands; Russia, subjected to US/EU economic sanctions as political punishment; and Iran, subjected to US/EU sanctions for exercising its sovereignty. Radical democracy alone will not be sufficient to repel these challenges. It will require alliances both from above and below to cement changes. We are many, but the few control the wealth, and have a military to back up that control.

A century ago, in 1913 to be precise, Lenin warned:

Oppression alone, no matter how great, does not always give rise to a revolutionary situation in a country. In most cases it is not enough for revolution that the lower classes should not want to live in the old way. It is also necessary that the upper classes should be unable to rule and govern in the old way.

We live in a very different world on many levels, but what the Russian revolutionary wrote a year before the outbreak of the First World War remains apposite.

Index